Practical AI Strategies

LEON FURZE

Practical AI Strategies

Engaging with Generative AI in Education

amba press

For Emily (again!)

Copyright © Leon Furze 2024

All rights reserved. No part of this book may be reproduced or transmitted in any form or by any means, electronic or mechanical, including photocopying, recording or by any information storage and retrieval system, without prior permission in writing from the publisher.

Published by Amba Press
Melbourne, Australia
www.ambapress.com.au

Editor: Rica Dearman
Cover designer: Tess McCabe

ISBN: 9781923116351 (pbk)
ISBN: 9781923116368 (ebk)

A catalogue record for this book is available from the National Library of Australia.

Contents

Acknowledgements ix
About this book xi
Introduction 1

Part 1: What is generative artificial intelligence? 3

Chapter 1   Generative artificial intelligence   5
Chapter 2   What is a prompt?   13

Part 2: Generative AI ethics 19

Chapter 3   Bias and discrimination   21
Chapter 4   Environmental concerns   24
Chapter 5   Truth and misinformation   27
Chapter 6   Copyright and intellectual property   30
Chapter 7   Privacy and datafication   33
Chapter 8   Human labour   36

Part 3: Assessment and school guidelines 39

Chapter 9   Beyond cheating   41
Chapter 10   The AI Assessment Scale   47
Chapter 11   Rethinking assessment for GenAI   52
Chapter 12   Australian Framework for Generative AI in Schools   70
Chapter 13   UNESCO guidelines   80
Chapter 14   Writing school guidelines   86
Chapter 15   Example academic integrity policy   92
Chapter 16   Do you need this application or platform?   96

Part 4: Practical strategies for GenAI — 103

Chapter 17	Planning	105
Chapter 18	Refreshing	111
Chapter 19	Improvising	115
Chapter 20	Personalising	119
Chapter 21	Collaborating	124
Chapter 22	Communicating	129

Part 5: Practical strategies for image generation — 133

Chapter 23	Critiquing	139
Chapter 24	Sketching	142
Chapter 25	Designing	144
Chapter 26	Visualising	146
Chapter 27	Storyboarding	148
Chapter 28	Creating	150

Part 6: The future of GenAI — 153

Chapter 29	Do we all need to be prompt engineers now?	157
Chapter 30	The future of multimodal GenAI	161
Chapter 31	Audio generation	164
Chapter 32	Video generation	168
Chapter 33	3D asset generation	171
Chapter 34	Code generation	173
Chapter 35	Bringing it all together	176

Conclusion	179
References	181
Further reading	183
GenAI apps and services	184
About the author	185

Acknowledgements

Since I wrote the previous two books in this series, *Practical Reading Strategies* and *Practical Writing Strategies*, there have been a few dramatic changes in my life, and in education. The biggest thanks go to my wife, Emily, who has supported me through a change in career, the first year of a new business and the start of my PhD. The kids have put up with a fair bit of disruption this year, too, even though (or maybe because) I've spent more time than ever working from home. I'd also like to thank my PhD supervisor, Dr Lucinda McKnight, who has been influential and supportive throughout the PhD so far.

Outside of my own little world, the education sector has been rocked again just as we were recovering from remote learning. I'd like to thank all of the schools, universities and educators I've worked with this year in navigating the chaos of generative AI. Special thanks to the English teacher community and Victorian Association for the Teaching of English (VATE) colleagues and members for being open to change and willing to test these ideas.

Finally, as always, thanks to Alicia, Rica and the Amba Press team for the *incredibly* fast turnaround getting this book out there – amazing team effort!

About this book

This is part disclaimer, part explainer and part guilty confession. ChatGPT was used to create some of this book. Shock! Horror! Disgust! *But not in the ways you might think…*

Since OpenAI kindly dropped ChatGPT on us from a great height in November 2022, there has been a lot of angst about cheating and plagiarism, which I'll write about in Part 2. In the interest of transparency, I think that, for now, it's helpful if people explain how they have used generative artificial intelligence (GenAI). In the future, the technology will be so ubiquitous we probably won't bother (imagine a disclaimer like this for *I have used spellcheck in Word…*).

I haven't relied on ChatGPT to write the content of this book or my blog posts, but that's mostly because I enjoy writing. But I do use ChatGPT and other GenAI tools daily, and that includes in the construction of this book. Here are some of the ways that GenAI was used in the process:

- I created a simple piece of software using ChatGPT that used a programming language called Python to 'scrape' my blog for articles in the *AI* category. The code took the content of those posts, stripped the website code and images, and copied them into individual Word documents. I then manually reorganised and edited those documents as the basis for many of the chapters in this book.
- I used another piece of code – also written in ChatGPT – to compile the final chapters into the draft manuscript. It saved me about six and a half minutes of copying and pasting.
- For the original articles and some of the new and updated chapters (including the final chapters), I recorded the drafts in a voice

memo and used Otter.ai to transcribe them, and GPT-4 to remove transcription errors and repetitions.
- I used ChatGPT and occasionally Claude for working out the tangles in some of my clunky and overwritten paragraphs. I tend to write how I speak, with lots of punctuation and enthusiasm, so most of those prompts were phrases like: *Take the following paragraph, and make sure it actually makes sense.*
- I have used image generation in various places. The AI Iceberg on page 10 is a Canva graphic, but most others were created in DALL·E 3 and Adobe Firefly.

Even for those mostly administrative tasks, I still feel a little uneasy writing 'I used ChatGPT while creating this book'. I think that's something we're all going to have to get used to.

Introduction

I applied for my PhD in 2022, interested in how large language models such as OpenAI's GPT-2 and GPT-3 might impact the ways we write texts. At the time, you could use OpenAI models as a developer by building an application on top of them, or through the OpenAI playground, which offered limited examples like a short story creator or grammar corrector.

Just a couple of weeks after the official start date of my PhD in November 2022, OpenAI released ChatGPT. The simple act of placing a chatbot interface on top of one of its most powerful models and releasing it for free to the public created a tremendous shift in how we interact with GenAI. Since then, there has been a lot of hype, but also some impressive developments in the field.

For educators, the release of ChatGPT also caused a fair amount of stress and anxiety. Media reports discussed the threat ChatGPT posed to traditional education, academic integrity and even writing disciplines. Universities in Australia and worldwide moved to pen and paper examinations to cope with the implications of this technology. Departments of education in most Australian states and territories banned ChatGPT, partly due to problematic terms and conditions, but also to address rising concerns over plagiarism and cheating.

In the following months, K-12 and tertiary education continued to grapple with the implications of these technologies for student use, particularly in generating texts for essays, topics and examinations. Yet despite academic integrity concerns, these technologies have potential positive and creative uses, including as assistive tech to support learners. Between November 2022 and November 2023, there were also significant advances in creative GenAI tools for multimodal purposes, including text, audio, video, image and code. This industry has moved incredibly quickly, outpacing education, government and the law.

Rather than focusing on ChatGPT or any other specific apps and services, this book takes a broader view of the technologies and explores ways educators might benefit from artificial intelligence (AI) in their day-to-day work. It aims to help educators learn to use the technology themselves, suggesting that the best way to learn is through experimentation using your own context and subject expertise.

The book is organised into six parts:

- Part 1 discusses how these technologies work, emphasising the importance of understanding GenAI, how models are constructed, where data comes from and how user input determines the model's output.
- Part 2 addresses the ethical concerns in GenAI, particularly those relevant to education. It encourages educators to engage in critical and reflective discussions about biases, intellectual property, privacy and data usage.
- Part 3 includes a discussion of guidelines and policies in schools, including a brief overview of the national and international education policy landscape.
- Part 4 introduces practical strategies for GenAI in education, focusing on text-based models like ChatGPT. It includes prompts and ideas applicable across various platforms.
- Part 5 follows this with a focused discussion of image generation, showing how it can be used in education and how it reveals biases and discrimination in AI.
- Part 6 explores multimodal GenAI, covering audio, video and code generation, and discusses the potential futures, challenges, risks and benefits of these technologies.

To get the most out of this book, read it with both an open mind and a critical eye. As with any digital technologies, GenAI is neither inherently positive or negative: it is the humans behind the technology that make ethical (or unethical) decisions. The advice in this book is designed to get you started with using GenAI, but also to encourage you to ask important questions about when and why we sometimes *shouldn't* rely on GenAI.

PART 1
What is generative artificial intelligence?

CHAPTER 1
Generative artificial intelligence

A brief history of artificial intelligence

Like any complex technology, artificial intelligence (AI) has its roots in several fields. From philosophy to computer science, mathematics to linguistics, tracing the history of AI and automation is a difficult business. The field was officially named in the 1950s, but ideas about automated machines have existed since long before then. This is a brief history of the development of AI from some of its earliest philosophical and theoretical inceptions through to modern-day technology.

Ancient automatons

Our fascination with automatons goes back a long way. Scholars have argued that the Ancient Greeks proposed automatic servants as a utopian alternative to human slaves in one of the earliest examples of technosolutionism I've seen yet. The myths of Daedalus, recalled by Plato and Socrates, describe the inventor creating 'animate statues'. Heron of Alexandria, in 60 CE, wrote about steam-powered automata, engines and wind turbines.

Skipping forward a few centuries, in the Byzantine Empire, King Constantinople VII hired craftsmen from Baghdad to create enthralling golden automata to impress his guests. Similarly, the Banū Mūsā brothers, a group of 9th-century Muslim inventors, created several variations of automata, including mechanical birds that could sing and move their wings.

In more recent history, the pace of invention and the passion for automata also accelerated. From Leonardo da Vinci's robotic knight in the 16th century to development of self-driving cars and advanced AI technology in the 21st century, we are obsessed with automation.

Although many of these inventions seem like vanity projects or interesting but useless distractions, the ideas that were generated alongside them – including advances in mathematics, engineering, philosophy and science – were incredibly important. Of all these inventions, one stands out as the obvious predecessor to modern computing: Charles Babbage's Difference Engine.

The impossible machine and the first programmer

Babbage's engines (Difference Engines number 1 and 2, and his Analytical Engine) represent some of the 'greatest intellectual achievements of the 19th century'. Although Babbage found it impossible to build his machines – due to the cost and the materials required – they did inspire the world's first computer programmer.

Ada Lovelace was the daughter of the famous poet Lord Byron, though her mother Annabella Milbanke Byron separated from her father and Ada never knew him. She first met Charles Babbage through a mutual friend in 1833. They exchanged ideas via correspondence and, even though it was never actually built, Lovelace wrote programs for the Analytical Engine, including an algorithm which could be used to compute the Bernoulli numbers.

The first AI summer

Although these early pioneers experimented with automation and even suggested some of the elements of modern computers, it was not until 1950 that we saw the beginnings of the field we now call AI. In his paper, 'Computing Machinery and Intelligence', Alan Turing proposed a test to determine the likelihood of a machine being capable of intelligence. The 'imitation game' – now more commonly known as the Turing Test – pits a machine against a human. To pass the Turing Test, a machine must be able to engage in a conversation with a human evaluator and convince the evaluator that it is a human, rather than a machine. Turing's work became one of the cornerstones of computer science.

In 1955, at a Dartmouth College conference, John McCarthy coined the term 'artificial intelligence' to describe a new field which brought together computer science and mathematics, including the work of other conference attendees such as Claude Shannon, famous for Information

Theory, and Marvin Minsky, who co-founded Massachusetts Institute of Technology's Artificial Intelligence Laboratory.

The period 1956–1973 is referred to as the 'first AI summer' due to an increase in research, funding and government interest in the studies of AI. During the period, there were many notable achievements, including the invention of ELIZA, the first chatbot, and the creation of LISP by John McCarthy, a programming language which is still in use today.

The period came to an end in 1973 when the *Lighthill Report* cast damning aspersions on the potential for AI researchers to achieve some of their grandest claims, including modelling the human mind.

What's in a name?

The term 'artificial intelligence' fell out of favour after the *Lighthill Report*, but that doesn't mean the field disappeared. Research into machine learning (ML), neural networks, natural language processing and other areas continued throughout the 1970s and 1980s.

Although 'AI' had become associated with the hype and unfulfilled promises of these earlier technologies, there were still great strides forward. From advanced mathematics like hidden Markov models to computer science and Kunihiko Fukushima's Convolutional Neural Networks, development continued towards the kinds of AI we are more familiar with today.

In the 1980s, AI entered a brief 'second summer' with the promise of neural networks, but couldn't shake the disappointments of previous eras. Despite efforts by researchers and technology companies, the field entered a second winter and research once again became more conservative.

Garry Kasparov versus the machines

It wasn't mathematics or computer science that ultimately lifted AI out of its second winter and back into the public eye: it was chess. Garry Kasparov's book, *Deep Thinking*, details the long and complicated journey towards the development of IBM's Deep Blue, the AI that was the first to beat a human chess Grand Master.

Since then, Deep Blue hasn't been the only AI to grab headlines by beating humans at their own games. IBM's Watson beat human contestants at *Jeopardy!* in 2011; Google's AlphaGo defeated a human Go champion in 2015; and in 2022, Meta's CICERO model defeated humans in a game of Diplomacy.

The modern age of AI

Over the past two decades, there has been a significant increase in funding and research for AI and ML projects. The rapid advancement of technology, such as smartphones, the internet and social media, has enabled leading tech companies, such as Google, Microsoft, Amazon and Meta, to develop powerful AI systems that drive their predictive engines, search tools and business models. These companies have access to vast amounts of data, which is crucial for ML algorithms.

In the early 1980s, the shift from symbolic methods to neural networks marked the beginning of the current AI revolution. With the availability of massive datasets and mass surveillance, these algorithms have become truly useful. As a result, AI can now be found in a variety of everyday technologies, ranging from cars to refrigerators. Despite controversies surrounding the definition of AI as intelligence, it is unlikely at this stage that we will experience another full AI winter.

The future of AI remains uncertain. While some experts worry about the potential harm that artificial general intelligence (AGI) or artificial superintelligence (ASI) could cause to humanity, others, such as futurist Ray Kurzweil or OpenAI CEO Sam Altman, are optimistic about the positive impact that AI could have on society. There is a growing consensus among experts that finding a balance between the dystopian and utopian perspectives of AI is crucial.

Current AI models, such as OpenAI's GPT and Google's PaLM and Gemini (the basis for its Bard chatbot), are dominating the headlines. Microsoft has built its Copilot products on top of the GPT model, and open-source models like Meta's Llama continue to grow in both popularity and sophistication.

AI has had a long and complex history since the term was coined in the 1950s, but there is no doubt that we are in a time of rapid development and change. The AI arms race between huge corporations like Google and Microsoft will accelerate the pace. As educators, we need to make sure we don't get swept up in another cycle of AI hype and lose sight of the very real ethical and social concerns of these technologies.

What is GenAI?

Generative artificial intelligence (GenAI) is a subfield of AI in which ML is applied to large datasets in order to learn ways to generate new data.

That data might be in the form of text, code, images, audio or anything else that can be turned into machine-readable content. In practice, that means that GenAI models are *multimodal* and can both read and create data in a variety of modes, such as text generation, audio (like speech-to-text), and even video and 3D assets.

While it's not necessary for every educator to have a full technical understanding of how GenAI models work, it is useful to know some of the details so that you can understand the strengths and limitations of the technology. Understanding how models are constructed helps to understand why they fabricate information (often called 'hallucinations') and why they can't be used as search engines. It also highlights why bias and discrimination are features of these models, which is explored more in Part 2.

The AI Iceberg

To help understand how large language models (LLMs) like GPT are constructed, I use the analogy of the AI Iceberg.

Picture an iceberg floating in the ocean. The visible part above the waterline is relatively small compared to the massive structure hidden beneath the surface. Now, imagine that this iceberg represents an LLM, like GPT-3 or 4, with its different components distributed above and below the waterline.

The dataset: underwater bulk

The bulk of the iceberg, hidden underwater, represents the vast dataset on which the LLM is trained. This data forms the bedrock of the model's knowledge and capabilities. It's vast and mostly unseen during any interaction with the model, but it's always there, informing every output.

Different models are trained on different combinations of datasets. For companies like OpenAI and Google, some of that information is proprietary. While we have some information on GPT-3's training data, GPT-4 is more of a mystery, and Google's PaLM is off-limits. But we do know a little about the kinds of data these large models are trained on. We know, for instance, that they contain data from sources like the Common Crawl, the Pile, Wikipedia and coding site GitHub. They are also trained on social media sites like Twitter and Reddit.

The dataset is *huge*. GPT-4, for example, is trained on around 13 *trillion* tokens – words or parts of words converted to machine-readable format. That's about 1,600 times the population of Earth.

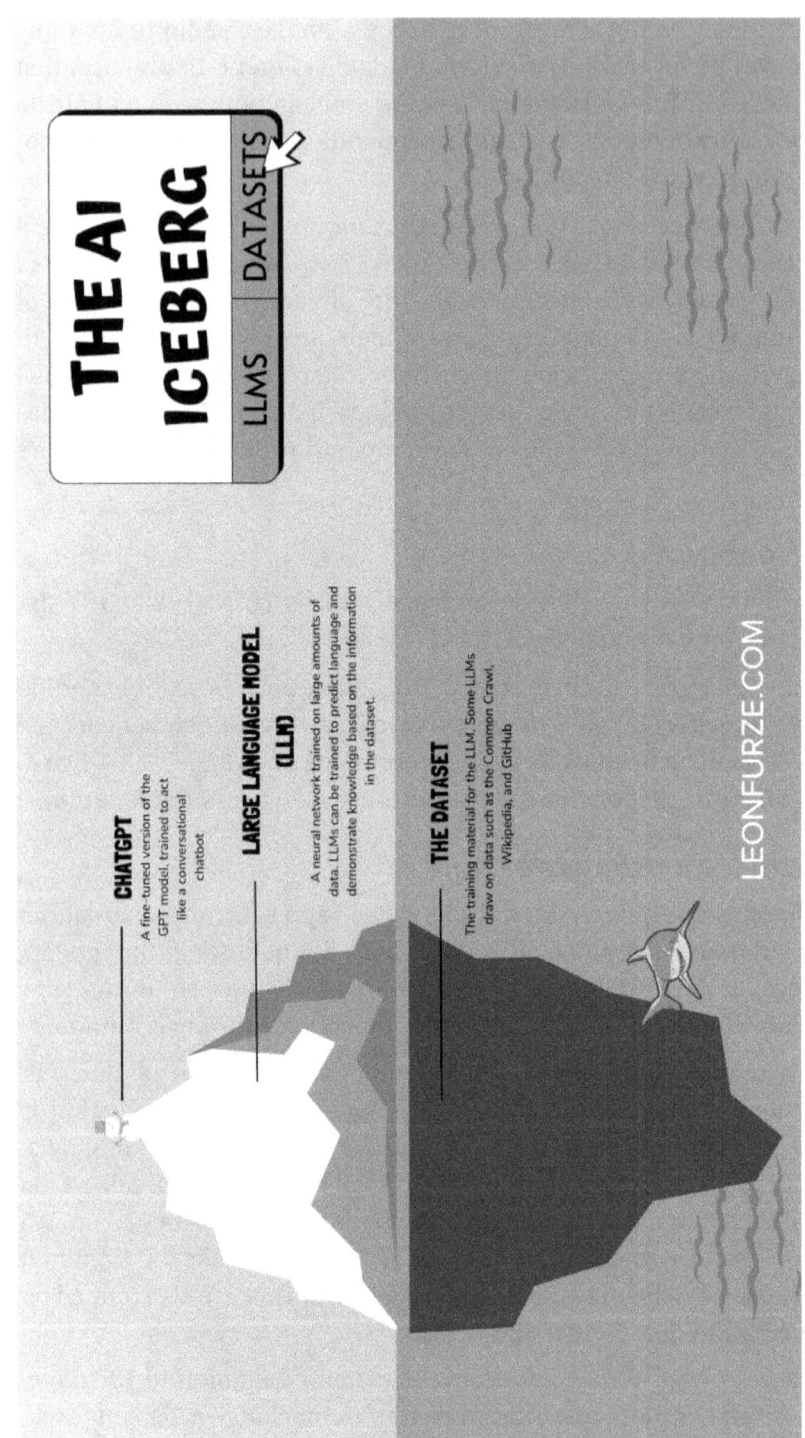

Figure 1: The AI Iceberg

The LLM: above the waterline

Emerging above the waterline is the LLM itself, the result of the training process fuelled by the vast dataset beneath. This visible portion is what we interact with when we use applications built on top of the LLM.

An LLM is an AI system that has been trained to understand and generate human language, including multiple languages and dialects, and code. These models are designed to predict the likelihood of a certain word given the words that came before it in a sentence or text. This ability allows them to generate coherent and contextually appropriate sentences, paragraphs and even entire texts.

Here's a *very* brief overview of some of the key processes:

Tokenisation

The text in the dataset is *tokenised*, which means it is broken down into machine-readable numerical code.

Weighting

The connections between tokens in the neural network are weighted, assigning numerical values for the probability of them occurring near to one another.

Transformer architecture and the attention mechanism

The Transformer architecture, introduced by Google researchers in 2017, allows the model to 'zoom out' and pay 'attention' to larger groups of tokens, representing entire phrases, sentences, and so on.

During this process, the model 'learns' the rules of language by associating words with other words, and predicting what the output should be based on the user's input (the *prompt*).

The most talked-about LLM right now is OpenAI's GPT, currently in version 3.5 (free) or 4 (subscription or access via Bing and the developer API). But there are many more out there, some open source, and some owned by companies like Google.

Applications like ChatGPT: the snowman

Finally, picture a snowman sitting on top of the iceberg. This represents an application like ChatGPT, which is built on top of the general LLM. The snowman is a more specialised figure carved from the raw material of the iceberg, just as ChatGPT is a version of the GPT model that has been fine-tuned specifically for conversational tasks.

The chatbot is trained to act as a 'helpful assistant' through various processes, including *system messages*, which are the rules passed to the model for every interaction, and reinforcement learning from human feedback (RLHF), where humans train the model and judge its output as positive, negative, harmful, correct, incorrect, and so on. There are ethical complications with RLHF, which I'll discuss in Part 2.

CHAPTER 2
What is a prompt?

If you followed any of the initial wave of hype surrounding GenAI, you might have seen roles in 'prompt engineering' being touted as the next big career path for young people, and prompt engineering jobs being offered for ludicrously high salaries. As GenAI models continue to improve, prompt engineering decreases in importance.

There have been some influential research papers about how to write effective prompts, including one which demonstrated that if you ask the model to 'take a deep breath and think this through', you can get better results (Yang et al., 2023). But overall, there is no secret recipe for writing prompts.

As you'll see in Parts 3 and 4, the best way to get results from GenAI models is to know what you're looking for, express it in clear, natural language and expect to work back and forth with the model until you get the desired results. Remember, models are trained on an enormous dataset of natural language and learn the rules of languages through our (mostly online) interactions. This means that in most cases you should be able to get what you need by providing clear instructions. In other words, just ask.

There's no magic involved in prompting, but there are a few general tips that you might find useful:

1. Be precise
2. Check the facts
3. Iterate and improve
4. Role play
5. Remind, remind, remind
6. Provide context

1. Be precise

GenAI models can't think, and they can't second guess what you want them to produce. If you provide a generic prompt, you'll get a generic response. This extends to any form of writing, including essays, fiction and advertising copy. The more detail you can provide, the better the response you'll get back. For example, if you provide a prompt like, 'Write an essay about *Pride and Prejudice*', you'll almost certainly get a very basic five-paragraph essay with no textual evidence. But if you start to add detail to your prompt, you'll end up with much more specific results.

Add as much detail to your prompts as possible. It might help to imagine that you are explaining the task to someone who has no knowledge of what you're trying to do. This should be something that teachers in particular excel at. For an analytical response, for example, this might include word length, topic, notes on tone and style, and specific requests on how to incorporate evidence. It still won't necessarily get all of that right, but you'll be off to a much stronger start.

2. Check the facts

GenAI models are notorious for fabricating information. The reason behind the nonsense generation stems from the way models construct their outputs. Remember: the model isn't thinking rationally, nor is it capable of fact-checking its own output. It is generating *predictions* based on the rules in the dataset.

When writing prompts, be specific in your requests for evidence, and always require the AI to provide a reference list so that you can manually check each source. Many models, including the paid version of ChatGPT and Microsoft's free Bing Chat, have an internet connection which can be used to 'ground' the response. They're not foolproof, though, and you should always check your facts. Remember: the machine doesn't think, but you do.

3. Iterate and improve

It's unlikely you'll get something perfect on your first attempt, no matter how much context you provide, or what directions you give in the prompt.

There is a tendency for chatbots to wobble off-course or misinterpret instructions. It pays to be patient, and to remember that even if it takes a few attempts, you're possibly still getting results faster than using GenAI-free methods.

It can also pay to keep track of your most successful prompts, either by going through the history feature of models like ChatGPT or Claude, or sharing, copy/pasting, or otherwise exporting your chats. Experiment, and learn what tactics work best for your needs.

4. Role play

One of the first things that 'the internet' did to ChatGPT was find ways to jailbreak it, causing it to act in unintended ways. This included tricking GPT into giving detailed instructions on how to hotwire cars, or for producing other such risky content. The most common of these approaches was very simple: ask it to play a role.

Asking ChatGPT to role play (or act, or pretend, or conduct a thought experiment) can also be a useful tool for crafting your prompts. If you're looking for a specific style of outcome, or trying to target a particular audience, then asking it to role play adds an extra layer of interest to the output.

When using role-play prompts, you can ask for personality traits (critical, cheerful, respectful, cynical), roles (teacher, school leader, student) and assign tasks to the model. You'll see many of these examples in Part 3.

I'd advise against the kinds of prompts where you attempt to get a language model to play the role of a real person, living or dead. I think it's disrespectful, and there is also no way that a language model can capture the complexities of another human.

5. Remind, remind, remind

Most chatbots have a 'memory'. It's this function which means you can 'teach' the model to correct errors, fix issues with its tone and style, and hold something like a realistic conversation. The memory is determined by the token limit of the model, which is the combined lengths of your prompts and the model's responses, plus any additional information you upload for context (for example, PDFs).

This token limit is continually increasing, but the memory only extends so far, and the tendency of chatbots is to 'forget' certain aspects of your prompt as it drifts back to its default style. This means that if you ask it to role play Socrates, for example, it will begin by assuming its approximation of the philosopher's worldview, but will eventually lose the thread.

The simplest remedy is to append a reminder to each prompt, just as 'in your role as Socrates' or 'because you are Socrates'. As the technology continues to advance and token limits increase, these memory issues will likely diminish.

6. Provide context

Finally, you might run up against another of GenAI's inherent flaws: it doesn't actually know everything (or anything, depending on how you define knowledge…). Anyone who has played around with ChatGPT will have encountered the bland "as a large language model trained by OpenAI, I only have access to…" style response. The dataset only extends to a certain point, so asking questions about anything beyond that – or anything which isn't included elsewhere in the massive dataset – will yield unimpressive results or fabricated responses.

To get around this, you can contextualise your prompts in various ways. You might copy/paste in additional information, such as excerpts from a curriculum document. In browser-enabled chatbots, you might provide links or explicitly tell the chatbot to browse for answers. Increasingly, you can upload files as 'context' or a 'knowledge base', which then anchor the response further. And with enterprise-level models, a technique called retrieval augmented generation (RAG) can be used to tie the response to a set of documents, such as an organisation's internal policies.

Examples of good and bad prompts

You'll see plenty of examples of good and bad prompts in Part 3, but here are a few with some notes based on the advice above.

Detailed analysis prompt

 Bad: Write about climate change.

 Good: Write a 200-word paragraph on the impact of climate change on Arctic wildlife, focusing on polar bears. Use browsing and include three recent scientific studies as references and analyse how climate change affects their food sources.

Role-play prompt

 Bad: Tell me about the Renaissance.

 Good: Pretend you are a Renaissance artist. Describe a day in your life, focusing on your artistic process, the types of materials you use and your feelings about the changing cultural landscape of the time.

Fact-checking prompt

 Bad: List some facts about Mars.

 Good: Provide five detailed facts about Mars, including its atmosphere composition and surface conditions. Ensure each fact is backed by a credible scientific source.

Contextual prompt

 Bad: Discuss modern educational challenges.

 Good: Discuss the challenges faced by modern education systems in urban areas, particularly focusing on technology integration and socioeconomic disparities. Reference the latest educational research findings from 2023 based on an online search.

PART 2

Generative AI ethics

CHAPTER 3
Bias and discrimination

Algorithmic bias is one of the most pressing ethical concerns of AI. Algorithmic bias occurs when the data used to train AI systems reflects the biases and prejudices of society, resulting in discriminatory outputs.

ChatGPT is a prime example of an AI system that can suffer from algorithmic bias. As discussed in Part 1, it is built on top of an LLM trained on a massive dataset, including the Common Crawl, which contains more than 12 years' worth of web pages.

While these datasets give the models tremendous capabilities, they are inherently biased. Most of the English language content online is written by white, Western males. Indiscriminately scraping the internet for data also means the dataset can contain racist, sexist, ableist and otherwise discriminatory language. As a result, ChatGPT can produce outputs that perpetuate these biases and prejudices.

AI models can also amplify the biases and prejudices of society as a whole. Just like any other society, the online community underrepresents marginalised groups and overrepresents others. For instance, the prevalence of racism and bigotry on sources like Reddit and Twitter can bleed through the datasets and be reproduced in the output of AI models.

Algorithmic bias can also occur during the methods of training and reinforcement used when developing AI systems. For example, predictive policing systems used by law enforcement agencies in the US disproportionately target poor, Black and Latinx communities, reinforcing existing systemic biases.

There are some organisations and communities trying to counteract this tendency. BLOOM, for example, is a model trained by BigScience through a 'crowdsourced' dataset, which had ethical guardrails in place from its inception, including avoiding potential biased datasets. This dataset is called ROOTS and contains 1.61 terabytes of text, including 46 languages.

Unfortunately, although BLOOM may be less biased than GPT, the jury is out on whether the bias has been removed entirely. BLOOM is also significantly less powerful than a model like GPT or Google's LaMDA, and so it is less likely that people will use it as the basis for their own software.

Case study: Predictive policing in the United States

Predictive policing is the use of data analysis, ML and AI to predict where crimes are most likely to occur and who is most likely to commit them. It is used by law enforcement agencies to allocate resources and personnel, identify potential criminal suspects and prevent crime before it happens. However, there are concerns about the potential for bias and discrimination in predictive policing algorithms, as well as questions about the legality and ethics of using AI to predict criminal behaviour. Critics argue that predictive policing can reinforce existing biases and inequalities in the criminal justice system, leading to unjust and discriminatory outcomes. This is because the datasets often include biases which are a product of systemic racism, including police mugshot databases with an inordinate amount of Black people and people of colour.

In August 2016, a coalition of 17 organisations, including the American Civil Liberties Union, issued a statement expressing concern about predictive policing tools used by law enforcement in the United States. The statement highlighted the technology's racial biases, lack of transparency and other flaws that lead to injustice, particularly for people of colour. The statement called for transparency about predictive policing systems, evaluation of their short- and long-term effects, monitoring of their racial impact and the use of data-driven approaches to address police misconduct. The statement also emphasised the importance of community needs and the potential of social services interventions to address problems for at-risk individuals and communities before crimes occur.

Facial recognition technology poses special risks for historically marginalised communities. Recent studies demonstrate the technical inaccuracies in facial recognition models and highlight that they are systemic and biased against people with darker skin. Companies have announced actions to improve the accuracy of their facial recognition algorithms and the diversity of their training datasets, but the scope and effectiveness of such efforts vary across vendors.

There remains an ethical question of if or when it is appropriate to use facial recognition to address legitimate security concerns, regardless of its accuracy. Guardrails are needed to ensure more equitable use of enhanced surveillance technologies, including facial recognition.

CHAPTER 4
Environmental concerns

The environmental concerns of AI are less reported on than algorithmic bias, but are just as important. In this chapter I'll explore the impact of AI technologies on the environment and what AI developers are doing – or not doing – to mitigate those risks.

Extractive AI

Kate Crawford – researcher, author and leading AI scholar – refers to AI as an "extractive" technology. In her book, *Atlas of AI*, she compares the AI industry to mining, drawing comparisons between oil and precious metal extraction.

The use of rare earth minerals and metals in the manufacturing of electronic components is a crucial aspect of the development of AI. These materials are used in the production of components such as batteries, memory chips and processors. Lithium, for example, is a key component in the production of batteries used in devices such as smartphones, laptops and electric cars. Similarly, cobalt is a vital component of rechargeable batteries used in many portable electronics and electric vehicles, while copper is essential for wiring and other electrical components.

However, the extraction and refining of these materials are resource-intensive processes that have significant environmental impacts. The mining of rare earth minerals and metals can result in soil erosion, deforestation and water pollution. It can also lead to the displacement of local communities and the destruction of their habitats. The production of electronic components also generates a significant amount of greenhouse gas emissions, contributing to climate change.

The demand for these materials is expected to increase dramatically as AI technologies continue to develop and become more widespread. This increase in demand will only exacerbate the environmental impact of their extraction and use. It is therefore essential to find sustainable solutions that reduce the environmental impact of these processes.

The hidden costs of the cloud

Cloud computing relies on massive data centres and infrastructure that consume a significant amount of energy and produce waste. These data centres require constant cooling, lighting and other support systems to ensure the optimal performance of servers and other hardware. The construction and operation of data centres also require huge amounts of energy, water and other resources, leading to carbon emissions and other forms of environmental damage.

One of the most significant environmental impacts of cloud computing is its contribution to climate change. The energy consumption of data centres is massive, and as more and more computing moves to the cloud, this demand will only increase. According to one estimate, the carbon footprint of the IT industry is 1.8–3.9% of global greenhouse gas emissions.

Many companies have pledged to make their data centres carbon-neutral or powered by renewable energy sources, but critics argue that these efforts are not enough. Offsetting carbon emissions or engaging in carbon trading does not address the underlying problem of energy consumption and waste production.

Case study: The carbon cost of training LLMs

Training a single LLM can emit as much carbon as five cars in their lifetimes (Strubell et al., 2019). The study estimated the energy consumption and carbon footprint of four popular LLMs: Transformer, ELMo, BERT and GPT-2. The results showed the most energy-intensive model was Transformer, which consumed 656,347kWh of electricity and emitted 626,155kg of CO_2 equivalent. This is equivalent to "nearly five times the lifetime emissions of the average American car". Another study has demonstrated that some image-generation applications can use the equivalent of a full phone charge of electricity per image (Luccioni et al., 2023).

Organisations like Microsoft, OpenAI and Google are investigating ways to reduce this impact, including:

- Choosing more efficient models or algorithms that require less energy or data to train
- Using pre-trained models or transfer learning techniques that leverage existing knowledge
- Reducing the frequency or duration of training sessions
- Using renewable energy sources or carbon offsets to power the training process
- Implementing best practices for data collection and processing
- Adopting ethical principles and guidelines for developing and deploying LLMs

It is worth bearing in mind that *all* digital technologies have an environmental impact. Google search, for example, uses a tremendous amount of energy every day. This is perhaps counterbalanced by the *reductions* in energy use that come because of digital technologies. For instance, being able to search for things online arguably reduces the energy cost of travelling (for example, to a library, school or university) to learn the same content. Similarly, AI technologies are being used to support research into the climate crisis, including powerful tools for modelling and predicting weather patterns or the impacts of pollution.

CHAPTER 5
Truth and misinformation

The concept of 'truth' is a significant ethical issue related to GenAI. Since the launch of ChatGPT in November 2022, there have been two primary concerns in the mainstream media: first, the likelihood of GenAI models generating false or fabricated content, and second, the potential for individuals to exploit them for dishonest purposes, including academic cheating and intentional dissemination of false information. Because academic integrity is such a concern in education, I've devoted a separate chapter to that in Part 3.

In this chapter, I'll explore both the GenAI tendency to fabricate information, and the various ways humans might misuse the technology.

Synthetic mirages

The first of these concerns – usually called 'hallucinating' – is a result of many different factors, including:

1. **Training data limitations:** The models are trained on large datasets containing text from various sources, which may include inaccuracies, biases or outdated information.
2. **Inability to verify facts:** AI language models lack the ability to fact-check or verify information. They rely on patterns and associations found in their training data and may generate false information if the data contains inaccuracies.
3. **Ambiguity in prompts:** If a user provides a vague prompt, the AI model might generate responses that are not accurate. The model tries to infer the user's intent based on the given input, but it might fail to do so correctly.

4. **Over-optimising for fluency:** AI models like GPT-4 are designed to generate human-like text, which can sometimes lead to them prioritising fluency over accuracy. As a result, the model may produce text that sounds plausible, but is a hallucination.
5. **Lack of a 'ground truth':** AI language models don't possess a deep, grounded understanding of the world like humans do. They work based on statistical patterns in data, which can sometimes lead to generating information that doesn't make sense or is incorrect.

In addition to perpetuating biases and discrimination, AI hallucinations pose a genuine risk of causing harm. The convincingly fabricated information produced by these models can infiltrate media, academic research and educational materials. An inattentive user might unintentionally incorporate this false content into various contexts, creating further issues.

AI and truth

Misinformation, disinformation and mal-information are false or misleading pieces of information that spread through social media, news outlets or word of mouth, often causing confusion and harm.

AI has become a tool in the viral spread of these types of information. Deepfakes – AI-manipulated videos and images – can deceive users with startling accuracy, making it harder to distinguish between fact and fiction. Platforms like TikTok have become incredibly problematic for the spread of misinformation, with algorithms powered by predictive AI creating 'filter bubbles' that expose users only to information that confirms their pre-existing beliefs, further amplifying false narratives.

Case study: Language models and the spread of fake news

Research conducted by Georgetown University, OpenAI and Stanford Internet Observatory (SIO) highlights the dangers of LLMs and the potential for them to manipulate public viewpoints (Goldstein et al., 2023).

The concern is that LLMs can be used to produce fake news and impersonate real individuals or organisations. The researchers used the

'ABC' model of disinformation to examine how LLMs can be misused. The model breaks down the various aspects that contribute to the escalation of false information. 'A' refers to 'Actor', which can be a group of individuals who create and broadcast disinformation. 'B' stands for 'Behaviour', which refers to the strategies used to spread propaganda. Lastly, 'C' stands for 'Content', which is untrue information.

The research found that LLMs can be used to promote a hoax agenda and negatively influence people. Since LLMs can generate large amounts of text quickly, they can overflow the internet with false information, making it difficult for people to differentiate between what is true and what is wrong. Even the scale of the campaigns can be amplified with minimal costs, making manipulation harder to detect.

The researchers recommend that careful attention should be paid to the type and source of news to avoid misuse, and users and developers should ethically use the model. While LLMs are not inherently malicious, they have the potential to be wrongly used for manipulation and disinformation.

CHAPTER 6
Copyright and intellectual property

Copyright is a hugely contentious aspect of the current wave of AI, particularly in the field of AI image generation. As AI continues to advance and both artists and laypeople produce creative works, questions are cropping up about who owns the copyright to those works. With AI it's possible to create 'original' art, music and literature, but the line between what is human generated and AI generated is increasingly blurred.

Copyright is also an area which is rapidly developing, and at the time of writing in November 2023, there are several high-profile court cases yet to be resolved.

Copyright and image generation

Image generation has been the most public and most contentious aspect of AI and copyright. For a quick scan of how problematic the area is, you only have to do a quick Google search of whether AI artists can copyright their work. Here are some of the results accessed in mid-2023:

- *No, you can't copyright images made by AI, says the U.S. Copyright Office.*
- *U.S. Copyright Office says AI-generated images do not qualify for copyright protection.*
- *AI-generated art can be copyrighted, say US officials – with a catch.*
- *AI-created images lose US copyrights in test for new technology.*
- *AI art tools Stable Diffusion and Midjourney targeted with copyright lawsuit.*

In some cases, it's an outright "no". In others, it seems to be a "no, but…". And in the final example, it's a hard "no" with a side of litigation, as companies like Stability AI (behind Stable Diffusion) and Midjourney find themselves on the receiving end of lawsuits.

So, why is AI image generation so contentious? The primary reason is based on how these models are trained. In order to build an AI image generator, the developer must use millions or even billions of images. Stable Diffusion, for example, was trained on around 2.3 billion images. Many of these images have been 'scraped' from the internet without the consent of the original creators.

This leads to problems with attribution, and with the potential for these AI image generators to reproduce art in another artist's style. I'm sure you've seen examples already with AI-generated art in the style of Van Gogh or Rembrandt. However, it also applies to living artists and photographers whose work has been scraped from sites like ArtStation and Flickr. These scraping issues also extend to LLMs, where text data is scraped from online sources which may include copyright texts. Complicating the matter further, some models have been proven to contain entire datasets of copyrighted text. The 'Book 3' dataset contains more than 180,000 copyrighted books from living authors, and was used to train models like Meta's Llama and others (Reisner, 2023).

There's the additional problem of whether the current copyright laws extend to work created 'by a machine'. Although AI images are generated by a human controlling the input via the prompt, it has been argued that the actual image is created by the AI, and not the human. This throws a legal roadblock in the way of copyrighting AI art, writing, film and music.

The same human authorship requirement for copyright protection under the current US law means that an AI-generated writing is likely either a public domain work immediately upon creation or a derivative work of the materials the AI tool was exposed to during training – the text found in the dataset.

The ownership of the rights in such a derivative would depend on various issues, including the dataset for training the AI tool (of which there are many variations, depending on the model used), its components, and the similarity between any particular work in the training set and the AI work.

Case study: *Zarya of the Dawn*

In February 2023, the U.S. Copyright Office revoked copyright protection for images created using the AI-powered Midjourney image generator for the comic book *Zarya of the Dawn* and issued a new copyright registration covering only the text of the work and the arrangement of images and text. The justification for this decision was incomplete information in the original copyright registration, which failed to disclose that the images were created by an AI model.

The U.S. Copyright Office argued that the images in the work generated by Midjourney were not the product of human authorship and thus not copyrightable. Despite author Kris Kashtanova's claim that she had 'guided' the structure and content of each image, the U.S. Copyright Office argued that Midjourney, not Kashtanova, originated the "traditional elements of authorship" in the images.

Kashtanova's attorney argued that every aspect of the work was authored by Kashtanova, with Midjourney serving merely as an assistive tool. However, this argument was rejected by the U.S. Copyright Office, which provided additional analogies to explain why Kashtanova was not the creator of the images, including the idea of hiring a human to create images using descriptions and performing a text-based image search on the internet.

Kashtanova reacted to the letter by framing it as an overall win for AI-augmented artists. The ruling protects the comic book's story and the image arrangement, which "covers a lot of the uses for the people in the AI art community". However, she expressed disappointment that the U.S. Copyright Office did not agree to recognise her copyright of the individual images. Kashtanova believes the output of a GenAI model depends directly on the creative input of the artist and is not random – individual images produced by Midjourney are a direct expression of her creativity and are thus copyrightable.

The decision means that AI-generated imagery, without human-authored elements, cannot currently be copyrighted in the United States. The U.S. Copyright Office's ruling on the matter will likely hold unless it's challenged in court, revised by law or re-examined in the future. The decision may eventually be reconsidered as the result of a cultural shift in how society perceives AI-generated art, allowing for a new interpretation by different members of the U.S. Copyright Office in the future. AI-powered artwork is still a novel and poorly understood technology, but it is rapidly becoming a feature of digital art.

CHAPTER 7
Privacy and datafication

There are growing concerns about the impact of AI technologies on our privacy. AI systems are often 'black boxes', making it hard to understand how they arrive at their decisions and raising questions about transparency.

The use of personal data in AI training data and the potential for data breaches and cyberattacks also pose significant privacy risks to individuals and organisations. As discussed earlier, AI systems can perpetuate biases and have unintended consequences that violate individual privacy rights. This chapter explores these ethical concerns around privacy and AI, and presents a few questions to explore this area across a range of subjects.

Where does all that data come from? Developers of LLMs, such as ChatGPT, often scrape their training data indiscriminately from the web without paying any attention to individual rights. These models are trained on vast swathes of internet data, often including personal information collected without consent or used in violation of privacy laws. This raises concerns about the ethical implications of developing AI models that rely on data collected without regard for individual privacy rights.

The lack of transparency and accountability around the collection and use of personal data in AI development has been a longstanding issue. The vast amount of data required to train these models means that personal information is often collected without explicit consent or knowledge of the individuals affected. Critics argue that developers of LLMs prioritise the creation of powerful algorithms over individual privacy rights, and that the industry is not sufficiently regulated.

These concerns have landed OpenAI in trouble with European regulators, particularly under the General Data Protection Regulation (GDPR) laws. The Italian regulator issued a temporary emergency decision demanding that OpenAI stop using the personal information of millions of Italians included in its training data, citing a lack of legal justification for using people's personal information in ChatGPT. The GDPR rules protect the data of more than 400 million people across Europe and apply to personal data that is freely available online. The decision by the Italian regulator highlights the growing concerns around the development of large AI models and the use of personal information in training data.

In the United States, the federal privacy commission also investigated OpenAI in 2023, following a claim made against the company that it had been unlawfully using personal and private data.

As discussed earlier, AI systems also have the potential to perpetuate and amplify biases in data, leading to discrimination against certain groups or individuals. This is a serious concern when it comes to privacy, as these biases can lead to the exclusion or mistreatment of individuals based on their personal characteristics. It can lead to members of the public being surveilled based on skin colour, place of residence or other factors which are part of the data used when training the models. These concerns extend into many areas of the AI industry, including facial and affect (emotion) recognition.

The storage of personal data in AI training data is also a significant privacy concern. In the creation of these models, personal data has been collected without explicit consent or knowledge of the individuals affected, and there may be inadequate protections in place to ensure that this data is used ethically and responsibly. Data breaches and cyberattacks also pose a huge risk for AI systems. In mid-2023, OpenAI experienced a breach due to a bug in one of their code libraries, which revealed the first and last names and email addresses of ChatGPT Plus subscribers, along with financial details.

What is 'datafication'?

'Datafication' is a term used to describe how all aspects of our lives are being turned into datapoints. Whether through the collection of our likes, shares and ratings on social media and streaming apps, or through the harvesting of physical data from devices like smartphones and smartwatches, datafication is what powers AI. In the words of British data scientist Clive Humby, "Data is the new oil."

Datafication has become a defining characteristic of our modern world, as technology advances enable the collection, storage and analysis of vast amounts of data from nearly every aspect of our lives. While this process has led to numerous benefits, such as improved efficiency of services, better decision-making, and increased personalisation of products and services, it also raises significant ethical concerns.

Case study: EdTech surveillance during COVID

The case of surveillance in the educational sector, particularly during the COVID-19 pandemic, is a concerning example of the intersection between technology and privacy. As schools shifted to remote learning, more than 4 million Australian students were exposed to a new level of digital tracking and data collection. This unprecedented situation was highlighted by a detailed investigation conducted by Human Rights Watch into the usage of educational apps and websites across 49 countries and reported on by the ABC (Duffy & Stewart, 2022). The study revealed a worrying trend: 89% of the educational technology (EdTech) products used globally posed potential risks to children's privacy. In Australia, the situation was particularly concerning, with several EdTech products found to be sharing children's data with advertisers.

The issue here goes far beyond mere data collection. The educational tools requested access to students' contacts and locations, and monitored their keystrokes, sending this sensitive information to nearly 200 ad-technology companies. This practice raised significant questions about the balance between educational needs and privacy rights. Parents and caregivers, teachers and students had to rely on these tools to maintain educational continuity, often without being fully aware of or consenting to the extent of data collection and surveillance involved. In some cases, it was reported that the companies behind these tools did not adhere to their own privacy policies, adding a layer of complexity and mistrust to the situation.

The pandemic, a global crisis, necessitated rapid adaptations in education, but it also revealed many vulnerabilities in the digital infrastructure of learning.

CHAPTER 8
Human labour

When people think of AI, the image that often springs to mind is that of sentient machines or shiny metallic robots, a depiction heavily influenced by popular culture. This narrative, along with language around 'magical' or 'mythical' AI, tends to overshadow actual pressing ethical issues associated with AI development and usage. This chapter will explore the exploitation of human labour in AI development, including low-paid workers used for categorising and labelling data, and the impact of the AI infrastructure on human workers.

In the ongoing arms race towards creating autonomous AI systems, multinational technology corporations are relying on a lot of 'ghost work'. This term, coined by anthropologist Mary L Gray and computational social scientist Siddharth Suri, refers to labour carried out by a 'global underclass' of precarious workers. Occupying roles such as content moderators, data labellers and delivery drivers, these workers often come from poor backgrounds and perform critical tasks for the tech industry at low wages and under suboptimal working conditions.

The way AI functions leans heavily on methods like statistical ML and deep learning through artificial neural networks. Such methods necessitate vast quantities of data. To obtain this data economically, platforms like Amazon's Mechanical Turk have emerged, enabling 'crowd work', which involves breaking down large tasks into smaller units that can be handled by numerous workers.

The emergence of such platforms and data-labelling companies, however, has resulted in workers being treated like parts in a machine, rather than individuals with rights and needs. These workers are often subjected to constant surveillance and repetitive tasks, and face punitive measures for any deviation from their assigned work. The mental and physical toll can be considerable, especially for content moderators who are continuously exposed to traumatic content without adequate support systems in place.

This situation shines a light on a key issue in AI ethics: the exploitation of labour in the AI industry. It's a stark reminder that the journey towards creating autonomous AI systems is not as 'autonomous' as it appears. It's built on the labour of often exploited workers who, ironically, contribute to the development of AI systems that might eventually replace them.

Some avenues that have been explored to address these challenges include transnational worker organising efforts, research collaborations with workers and public accessibility of research findings. An essential aspect of this conversation is the role of solidarity between high-income tech workers and their lower-income counterparts. There's potential here for those with more influence within corporations to advocate for their colleagues who have less.

Case study: OpenAI's data labelling

OpenAI, the company responsible for the enormously popular ChatGPT, has made great strides in the past 12 months with many forms of AI. However, some of these achievements have raised significant ethical concerns regarding the exploitation of human labour and the handling of harmful content. This case study explores the findings of an excellent piece of investigative journalism published in *Time* magazine in 2023.

GPT-3 was designed to demonstrate exceptional linguistic abilities, stringing together sentences in a strikingly human-like manner. It was trained on hundreds of billions of words scraped from the internet, a vast corpus of human language that endowed GPT-3 with impressive language-processing skills, but also incorporated the internet's toxicity and bias.

To tackle these challenges, OpenAI aimed to construct an AI-powered safety mechanism, akin to the systems deployed by social media companies like Facebook to detect and remove hate speech and other forms of toxic language. The premise was straightforward: feed an AI with labelled examples of violence, hate speech and abuse, and this tool could learn to identify and eliminate these forms of toxicity.

In November 2021, OpenAI began the process of creating this safety system. It sent tens of thousands of snippets of text to an outsourcing firm in Kenya called Sama. The text was pulled from various internet sources, including extremely harmful content describing graphic situations of abuse, murder and self-harm. Sama, a company based in San Francisco, employs workers in India, Kenya and Uganda, to label data for Silicon Valley clients such as Google, Meta and Microsoft. While it brands itself as an 'ethical AI' company and boasts of lifting more than 50,000 people out of poverty, there are concerning elements surrounding its operations.

Sama's data labellers, who were contracted to work on behalf of OpenAI, earned a take-home wage of approximately $1.32 to $2 per hour depending on seniority and performance. This rate was for work that involved labouring over harmful, potentially traumatising content. To learn about the full extent of the trauma on these workers, you should read the original article at *Time* magazine (Perrigo, 2023).

The case of OpenAI's development of GPT-3 and its filtering process serves as an example of the ethical challenges that permeate the AI industry. As technology companies continue to pursue advancements in AI, it is critical to scrutinise the labour practices that underlie these developments and to ensure that the quest for 'ethical AI' does not overlook the wellbeing and fair treatment of the human workforce powering it.

PART 3
Assessment and school guidelines

CHAPTER 9
Beyond cheating

The initial launch of ChatGPT in November 2022 was met with a lot of media speculation and fear around students using the technology to cheat. This, along with the terms and conditions at the time, contributed to state- and sector-wide bans of the technology. At the time of writing, it's almost been 12 months since the release of ChatGPT and thankfully the bans have now been lifted in most jurisdictions in Australia. Unfortunately, the narrative of 'catching' students using GenAI persists, and educators in both K-12 and tertiary are still stuck in the loop of detection tools, pen and paper examinations, and 'proctoring' software, such as lockdown browsers, as methods to stop or monitor GenAI use.

This part of the book explores some of the reasons why GenAI shouldn't necessarily be considered cheating. It serves as a good starting point for approaching and developing school- and institution-wide policies and guidelines for GenAI.

Does GenAI plagiarise or copy?

One concern of these technologies has been that students using them are automatically plagiarising. This assumes that a model like ChatGPT 'copies' its answer from the dataset. In some respects, language models like GPT can generate responses which contain verbatim copies of text from the dataset. For example, in the following prompt I can easily get ChatGPT to tell me the opening line of a classic novel:

> Generate the opening lines of Pride and Prejudice.

It will also perform in the same way for more recent books that are still under copyright, such as JK Rowling's *Harry Potter and the Philosopher's Stone*.

However, if you push this much further, you'll get a response telling you that the model can't reproduce copyrighted texts, and sometimes telling you to go and purchase a copy of the original text. That's a trained response: the model has been 'taught' to respond with a comment like this when a user appears to be asking for something which might breach copyright. In other models without these guardrails, however, they can be prompted to provide verbatim responses, which seemingly recall text from the dataset.

But does that mean that these models are 'plagiarism machines'? It's a little more complex than that. These models work by analysing the dataset and learning the patterns of grammar, syntax, style, and so on, as explained in Part 1. As a result of the process, data that is repeated more often (such as the opening lines of famous books, or facts available and commonly repeated online) are more likely to appear in generated output. Technically, it's called *overfitting* and companies like OpenAI put in place measures to limit the problem, but it certainly still happens.

So, the answer to the question 'Does GenAI plagiarise or copy?' is 'Sometimes, but not in the ways you might expect.' It's therefore not possible to claim that a student's use of GenAI equals plagiarism. If a student uses GenAI to generate an essay, for example, then much of the response will be novel content, and any content that comes verbatim from the dataset is more of a side-effect than an intentional copy.

Is using GenAI cheating?

This depends on your definition of cheating, and on the task.

A student using GenAI to complete an entire task might be akin to contract cheating, where a person pays someone else to do the work for them. In fact, ChatGPT might even *reduce* the amount of actual contract cheating and put the contract essay writers out of work. There's not much difference between paying someone to write an essay and dropping the entire question into ChatGPT to generate the response.

The key factors in determining whether GenAI constitutes cheating include:
- Whether the use of GenAI is expressly forbidden
- Whether the use is required to be disclosed
- Whether there is a competitive advantage to be gained using GenAI

Essentially, 'cheating' is whatever we decide it is. If an educator decides to ban GenAI use, then of course any use is cheating. If a student uses the technology in a deliberately deceitful way, or to gain an unfair advantage, then it's cheating.

The problem, as I'll explain throughout this chapter, is that it's next to impossible to enforce strict anti-GenAI policies. If you consider GenAI use to be cheating, for whatever reason, you're going to have a hard time monitoring and evaluating student work outside of specific constraints.

Can't I just use detection software?

Hot on the tails of ChatGPT, GenAI 'detection' software started to appear in tertiary and then secondary education contexts. You can see the appeal. Just as a new technology arrives which threatens to hugely undermine assessment practices, a few helpful developers provide an easy way to catch students using GenAI.

Unfortunately, detection software doesn't work.

Many studies have demonstrated that detectors like GPTZero and Turnitin simply don't have the level of accuracy needed for an academic integrity judgement. Entirely human writing frequently scores about the same as the entirely GPT written text. After a very minimal re-prompt, GPT written content can even score as 'more human' than the human text.

Given the high-stakes nature of assessment in the tertiary sector, there is a lot of research going into detection software. The results aren't promising – more sophisticated LLMs like GPT-4 can beat detection tools. Detection tools have also been demonstrated to discriminate against English as an Additional Language (EAL) authors, flagging their writing as AI-generated more frequently.

What are the ethical issues of 'catching' and 'detecting'?

As pointed out above, detection tools have been demonstrated to be biased against non-native English writers. There are also other ethical considerations when trying to 'catch' or 'detect' GenAI use. Firstly, students who are more digitally literate – or more fluent in general – may be able to use the technology in more sophisticated ways to generate undetectable content. These students might, for example, be able to construct better prompts, which result in more 'human-like' output; or they may use some of their own writing in the prompt to produce generated text that is more similar to their real 'voice'.

Some students will also have better access to technology. This might simply mean device or internet access at home, or could mean access to more sophisticated models, such as the subscription-only GPT-4 model in ChatGPT. These students will produce content that evades detection software, much of which is trained to detect content from GPT-3 and 3.5.

Essentially, a student who is more confident, competent or has access to a higher-quality application might be able to 'cheat' and get away with it. This is part of the 'digital divide' (see page 81), but it is amplified when we consider that detection is more likely to be seen as an option for high-stakes, competitive tests where wealthier, more literate students already have an advantage.

What does all this mean for assessment design?

I'll begin this answer with a straightforward but possibly unpopular statement: for any unsupervised assessment, we have to assume students *might* use GenAI.

This isn't a statement about trust. I'm not suggesting, like some of the early headlines when ChatGPT was released, that all students are compulsive cheats. I'm stating that given the ubiquity, ease of access and inability to detect GenAI, there is simply no way to guarantee it won't be used for any assessment that doesn't happen under supervision. However, I'm also not suggesting that all assessment should be supervised, and certainly not conducted under exam conditions.

Here are a few considerations when designing assessments with GenAI in mind:

- Does the student need to demonstrate knowledge or competency without *any* use of GenAI? Are you sure? If so, conduct the assessment in person, under supervision. It's the only option.
- Is the assessment a practical or experiential task that doesn't benefit at all from the use of GenAI? I.e. is there really no way that GenAI could be used for the task? Think: fitness assessments, constructing a physical product…

- Are you assessing knowledge or skills? Can the skills be assessed in a real-world context, or applied to the student's personal opinions and experiences?
- Assuming students can and possibly will use GenAI to complete some or all of the task, are *all* students equally aware of the technology and do they have equal access? If not, what can be done to ensure that students with access to better models are not advantaged?
- If students 'opt out' of using GenAI, can you guarantee they won't be disadvantaged?
- Does the assessment need to be completed as a written task? Can it be completed orally, such as a discussion, viva, presentation, pitch or debate?

On page 47, I'll outline an AI Assessment Scale, which covers many of these areas and offers a way to discuss the appropriate use of the technology with students.

What about distance learning, online courses or out-of-class assessments?

I've spoken with school leaders from distance education providers, as well as tertiary providers with hundreds of online students. I also work with schools that offer programs like the International Baccalaureate, which includes an extended essay that is worked on over time, and often out of class. My answer here is the same: anything that happens outside of a supervised setting (which may be *everything*, in this case) can potentially be completed with GenAI. Proctoring software and lockdown browsers are as much of a dead end as detection tools and, unfortunately, create a culture of mistrust.

However, it might still be possible to engage students in rich, online discussions and conversations where their knowledge can be assessed in ways other than via a written response. Otherwise, you have to accept that students could be using GenAI. Refer back to the questions above about assessment design. How might tasks be structured so that it doesn't matter if students use GenAI, or so that there is no advantage in using it?

How can I authenticate student work?

First of all, assume that most students want to do the right thing.

If you have clear guidelines about academic integrity, and you avoid competitive behaviours that might lead to a culture of cheating, you make authenticating student work much easier.

Authentication can happen in a few ways:

- Complete certain stages of the assessment, such as planning, brainstorming, drafting or editing under supervision. Not necessarily under exam conditions – but in person and as part of the classwork. In fact, instead of calling this 'supervision', you might just say it's collaboration.
- Retain copies (physical or digital) of work completed along the way. Compare this work to the final submission.
- Discuss the work with students. It's often simple to see if a student really has the knowledge and skills or if they've been relying on something like ChatGPT to produce work for them.
- Lean on formative rather than summative assessment, providing more opportunities for students to demonstrate their own knowledge.
- Have clear guidelines for how to acknowledge the use of GenAI. Students might include links to chat transcripts, copies of prompts, screenshots or a simple acknowledgement of the app used.

Can a student really use GenAI in my task?

Probably.

Assuming there is some form of written component, or that the assessment is based on the students' knowledge of content, then it's highly likely that GenAI could be used to generate some or all of the response. If there are visual requirements, such as a folio of images, photos or even hand-drawn elements, then we will reach a time soon where this is possible through image generation, too.

We are already at the stage where a recorded oral can be easily faked using a platform like ElevenLabs or Descript. These services take a recording of a voice and generate a realistic – if occasionally robotic – facsimile of the original voice. As I mentioned earlier, we have to assume that students can and will use GenAI in some form or another in any out-of-class assessment.

CHAPTER 10
The AI Assessment Scale

This AI Assessment Scale arose from a conversation with the education faculty at Edith Cowan University in Perth, Australia. We were discussing the need to move beyond a binary yes/no approach to AI. That discussion led to this 'scalar' approach, which outlines ways for the technology to be used (or not used) as appropriate to the task.

It's important to note that this isn't necessarily an academic integrity tool – it's not used after the assessment to check whether students have used AI or to 'catch' or detect AI use. It's used before and during the development of the assessment alongside students to negotiate how and why the technology might be used in a given task. It's flexible enough to be adapted into many subject areas, and the levels themselves can be adjusted to suit the task.

The five levels of the AI Assessment Scale

The AI Assessment Scale ranges from 'no AI' to 'full AI' and encompasses different levels of AI integration. Here's a breakdown of the five-level scale:

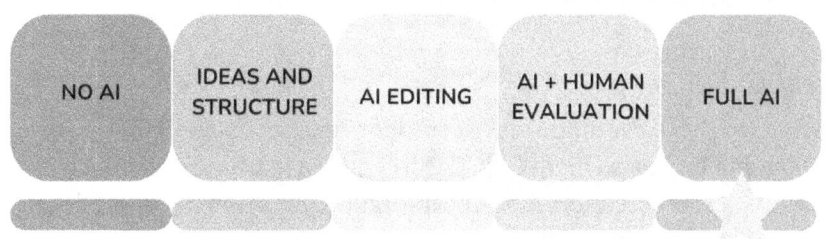

Figure 2: The AI Assessment Scale

Level 1: No AI
- Students can't use GenAI.
- Suitable for assessments needing personal skills/knowledge.
- Activities: technology-free discussions, in-class work, viva-voce exams.
- Recommended for supervised or low-stakes assessments due to equity concerns.

Level 2: AI-assisted ideas generation and structuring
- GenAI used for brainstorming and structuring ideas, but final work must be human authored.
- Useful for idea development and foreign language classes.
- Activities: collaborative brainstorming, creating structured outlines, research assistance.

Level 3: AI-assisted editing
- Students use GenAI for refining and editing their work.
- Beneficial for language improvements and multimodal content.
- Activities: correcting grammar/spelling, suggesting synonyms, structural edits, visual editing.
- Students submit original work alongside AI-assisted content for authenticity.

Level 4: AI task completion, human evaluation
- Students actively use GenAI for specific task components, critically evaluate AI outputs.
- Encourages understanding of GenAI's capabilities and limitations.
- Activities: direct AI generation, comparative analysis, critical evaluation, integrating AI content.
- Flexibility in AI and human intelligence interaction.

Level 5: Full AI
- AI used throughout the task at student/teacher discretion.
- Suitable for tasks where GenAI is integral to learning outcomes.
- Activities: co-creation, GenAI exploration, real-time feedback loops, creating GenAI products.
- Encourages exploring GenAI as a collaborative and creative tool.

Benefits and challenges of incorporating AI into assessments

Incorporating AI into assessments could yield several potential benefits, such as enhancing the creativity, writing quality and efficiency of feedback processes and self-assessment. However, there are also challenges to consider.

Ensuring that AI does not replace students' critical thinking and problem-solving skills is crucial, and something which I know from experience many parents and caregivers are concerned about. The ethical concerns around AI-generated content and balancing the use of AI with traditional assessment methods must be addressed.

Applying the AI Assessment Scale to non-writing tasks

The AI Assessment Scale could easily be applied to other types of assessments, such as oral presentations, group projects and problem-solving tasks. Furthermore, it can be applied to other AI applications like image generation, data analysis and virtual simulations. In each case, educators can use the five-level scale to determine the appropriate level of AI integration.

Think about how this scale could be applied to a Visual Arts assessment, for example. Students might use no AI in the initial idea generation, and then supplement their brainstorming with an image-generation app to look for inspiration – much in the same way they might already use apps like Pinterest. They could create digital artwork themselves, with the use of AI, or using AI to entirely generate the artwork and then editing it themselves.

Creating clear guidelines for AI use in assessments

The idea behind the AI Assessment Scale isn't to 'catch' students in the act of cheating. The scale should be used as a discussion point, and maybe as an addition to a task sheet to clearly indicate how students are permitted or encouraged to use AI for a given assessment.

It might also be appropriate to break a task down into different elements, and apply different levels of the scale to different parts of the assessment.

For example:

- Your initial brainstorming must be done by hand, on paper, using your knowledge and ideas only. (Level 1)
- Your ideas can then be refined and developed using AI and a thinking routine like Generate-Sort-Connect-Elaborate. (Level 2)
- Once you have developed your initial ideas, your first draft outline should be completed by hand in class. (Level 1)
- You may use AI to expand on your outline and suggest improvements to clarity, logic and the overall structure. (Levels 3 and 4)
- Once you have completed your draft writing, you may use AI to proofread and make recommendations. (Level 3)

Using ChatGPT with the Assessment Scale

Finally, here are a few examples of how a student might approach an assessment task using prompts in ChatGPT.

No AI (Level 1)

- Sorry, no prompts here!

Brainstorming and ideas (Level 2)

- Generate a list of features that a teenager might be looking for in a smartphone app that helps them track their environmental waste.
- Here are three of my ideas about <topic>: <copy/paste ideas>. Add onto each of those ideas with three connected ideas each.

Outlining and notes (Level 2)

- These are my notes from a lesson on <topic>: <copy/paste notes>. Turn them into an outline for an essay on the question <question>
- This is a transcript of an audio brain dump. Turn the transcript into organised notes with headings and subheadings: <copy/paste transcript>

Feedback and editing (Level 3)

- Role play: You are my secondary school Year 12 English teacher. You haven't had your morning coffee. Provide some brutally honest feedback about the quality of my arguments: <copy/paste draft>
- Check the grammar, spelling and punctuation of this and make recommendations: <copy/paste draft>

AI + human evaluation (Level 4)

- Generate a draft critique of this article: <upload or copy/paste article>. (Student then 'critiques the critique'.)
- Analyse this image and provide a detailed discussion of the style, structure, composition, framing, use of persuasive device, etc. (Student writes their own analysis and compares/contrasts with the AI output.)

Full AI (Level 5)

- This is the audio transcript of a group discussion on <topic>. Use it to generate the outline for a PowerPoint presentation, and the outline for a report.
- Use the outline for the report you created to write the full report. Begin with the first section and wait for our feedback.

Going further with the AI Assessment Scale

I originally designed the AI Assessment Scale with K-12 in mind and focused it on writing tasks. While the original version did include some ideas for use in other disciplines, it took around six months to flesh out. Over the course of 2023, I worked with Dr Mike Perkins, Dr Jasper Roe and Dr Jason MacVaugh at British University Vietnam to extend the AI Assessment Scale into a tertiary context and make it truly useful across disciplines. The scale reproduced in this book is based on that work.

You can check out the complete paper on the updated AI Assessment Scale and the process we went through on arXiv by searching for *Navigating the generative AI era: Introducing the AI assessment scale for ethical GenAI assessment* (Perkins et al., 2023). The paper includes a detailed discussion on academic integrity and the rationale for the scale, as well as supplementary materials with examples in many disciplines.

CHAPTER 11
Rethinking assessment for GenAI

This chapter explores some of the ways we might rethink assessment to account for GenAI. There's nothing particularly revolutionary or new here: alternatives to essays, using oral discussions and 'ungrading' have all been around since long before GenAI. But we've come to rely on written assessments – and particularly essays – to assess knowledge in many disciplines, and GenAI might mean we have to rethink that.

Beyond essays

There are plenty of good reasons to use the essay as a formal piece of assessment. Essays offer an opportunity for students to demonstrate their knowledge in a cohesive, structured manner, forming logical arguments and leading the reader through their thoughts. They can also be creative and playful, allowing a confident writer to express their unique authorial voice.

Essays are also relatively easy to grade, and scalable. It's straightforward enough to collect and mark essays conducted under examination settings, even from thousands of students. Every year, the Victorian Curriculum and Assessment Authority (VCAA) collects around 45,000 English essays, which are scanned into Pearson's eMark platform and distributed to a few hundred assessors. It's a huge task, but not unreasonable, and the essays are accurately graded in a two-week period.

Unfortunately, the expediency of essays as a form of assessment has made the form a 'go to' in many subject areas and at various levels from primary through to tertiary. Don't get me wrong, I personally love writing. I'd take an essay over a multiple-choice exam any day, and I'd probably prefer to write than undertake an oral exam. But the problem is, not everyone enjoys writing, and not everyone can write an extended response.

The answer, however, doesn't lie in banning GenAI or locking down all essays to examination conditions. Exams are terrible for accessibility, cause anxiety and are far from a genuine representation of most skills. Instead, we need to look for ways to move beyond the essay. Aside from the 'threat' of GenAI chatbots, here are a few more reasons why you might want to look beyond an essay or long written response as a primary form of assessment:

- **Limited scope:** Essays often focus on individual performance and intellectual capability, which may overlook other important skills, such as teamwork, verbal communication or practical skills.
- **Time-consuming:** Writing, revising and grading essays can be time-consuming for both students and educators.
- **Writing skills bias:** The format may unfairly favour individuals with strong writing skills, even if the subject matter does not primarily concern writing ability.
- **Plagiarism risk:** Essays can be susceptible to plagiarism, which undermines the learning process and the integrity of the assessment.
- **Stress-inducing:** Some individuals might find essay writing to be stressful or anxiety-inducing, especially if they struggle with articulating their thoughts in writing.
- **Fixed interpretations:** Essays often require adherence to a particular thesis or argument, which may discourage the exploration of alternative perspectives or creative thinking.
- **Cultural bias:** The conventional essay format may reflect a particular cultural or academic tradition that might not be inclusive of, or accessible to, all learners.
- **Subjectivity in grading:** Grading essays can be subjective, and variations in grading standards can affect fairness and consistency in assessment.
- **Limited feedback:** In large classes, providing detailed, constructive feedback on essays can be challenging, which may hinder the learning process.
- **Misalignment with learning objectives:** If the primary learning objectives are to assess practical skills, collaborative abilities or other non-writing-related competencies, essays may not be the best assessment tool.

The alternatives

Let's take a look at a few alternatives which directly address those concerns, and which might also mitigate the risk of students breaching academic integrity by using GenAI in unacceptable ways. For each of the assessment types I'll provide an overview and then some examples. Since I haven't taught in every single subject area, some of the examples will be generated by GPT-4.

Performance based

If you've ever taught in Australia's Vocational Education and Training (VET) sector, you'll find many of the assessment types in this chapter familiar. That's because performance-based tasks, observations and on-the-job skills are par for the course in vocational education. But there's no reason this can't transfer to any secondary or tertiary subject. After all, any discipline should be preparing students to use the skills and knowledge in some real-world context, whether that's further study, employment or another field entirely. Even esoteric subjects like philosophy or subjects in the creative arts where the 'goal' isn't necessarily tied to economic imperatives require students to develop skills they'll actually use in the future. For core subjects in secondary – Maths, English, Science and the Humanities – the skills and knowledge are far better related to real-world applications than abstract chunks of knowledge.

Performance-based assessments may require students to respond to essential questions and demonstrate skills in a real-world scenario. They allow for interdisciplinary knowledge and don't necessarily rely on the content taught in each unit or topic.

Here are a few examples:

1. **Mathematics:** Students could be tasked with designing a budget plan for a small start-up, applying mathematical principles to allocate resources, project profits and manage expenses. The final presentation could include a detailed report and a presentation to a mock panel of investors.
2. **English:** Students might be asked to create a multimedia storytelling project where they write and illustrate a short story, then present it to a younger age group at a local library or school.

This task encourages creative writing, visual storytelling and public speaking skills.

3. **Physical Education:** Create a fitness programme for a specific goal such as preparing for a 5km run or improving general health. Students could track their progress, reflect on their experiences, and present their results and learnings to the class.
4. **Economics:** Students could be assigned to analyse the economic impact of a recent local or global event using economic theories and models. They could present their findings in a video essay format to be shared with the community, encouraging real-world application and public discourse.
5. **Italian (LOTE):** Students could be tasked with planning and executing an 'Italian Culture Day' event, where they prepare Italian dishes, present on various aspects of Italian culture and engage in conversations in Italian. This task encourages language use in a practical, engaging and collaborative context.

Portfolio or writing journal

I love writing journal tasks. They're my recommended form of assessment for creative writing tasks where students are required to demonstrate skill development over time. Portfolios of artwork, design ideas and creative writing are common, but this assessment approach can be applied to other disciplines and subjects. When I go through my own notes for my PhD confirmation document, it looks very much like a writing journal. I have annotations, extended abstracts, short snippets of writing which may or may not make it to the final piece and draft versions of the document itself. Each piece contributes to the whole of my knowledge on the subject. The problem is, in secondary and tertiary education, we often don't value the whole journey.

Obviously, my situation is different; if you're studying at this level, you have to really want to. It's not like secondary English, where you're doing it because it's compulsory, or even undergraduate studies where you might be doing it just to get a job or because it's expected. But if both students and educators at every level could learn to value the process of writing and creating, then we would probably find there's a lot more valid content to assess than just the finished product. The added bonus is you'll get a lot more insight into the student's usual style, voice and way of thinking, which can be useful in academic integrity conversations.

Here are a few examples outside of the usual subject areas of visual arts and English:

1. **Physics research journal:** Students could maintain a journal documenting their investigations into various physics phenomena. They could conduct small experiments, record observations, analyse data and draw conclusions over the course of the term or semester. Additionally, they might reflect on how their understanding evolves with each experiment and how the concepts relate to real-world applications.
2. **Business management case study portfolio:** Students could create a portfolio of case studies analysing different businesses or management scenarios. For each case, they could provide an overview, identify challenges, propose solutions based on management theories, and reflect on the potential outcomes and lessons learned. This portfolio could showcase their analytical, problem-solving and strategic thinking skills.
3. **Geography field study journal:** Students could document field studies investigating local geographical issues or features. They could record observations, collect data and analyse findings in a journal, reflecting on the implications and how the local findings connect to broader geographical concepts.
4. **Psychology observational journal:** Students could maintain a journal where they observe and analyse human behaviour in various settings, relating their observations to psychological theories and concepts. They might also reflect on how these observations alter or deepen their understanding of psychological principles.
5. **History investigation portfolio:** Students could conduct investigations into different historical events or figures, documenting their research process, sources, analyses and reflections in a portfolio. They might also include essays or reports that synthesise their findings, showcasing their ability to engage with historical inquiry and analysis.

Remember, with this type of assessment there's no need to have a 'finished product' at the end. Students can, of course, adapt their separate pieces of work and write a final essay, but they don't have to.

Project based

Project-based learning (PBL) is nothing new. Some schools and education institutions have entire curricula based on PBL, dedicated middle-years programs or whole sites devoted to the format. You don't have to go all in on PBL, though, to get some of the benefits of project-based assessment. In a typical project-based assessment, there is a real-world problem and a structure like a design thinking process. There may also be an inquiry problem or research topic, and the project extends over a number of weeks or even a whole term or semester. At the end, there is often an opportunity to present or pitch an idea or solution to the problem.

As a means to rethink assessment in light of GenAI, project-based tasks could be a great option as they are engaging, authentic and allow a student to demonstrate their skills in a broad range of tasks rather than a pass/fail scenario. Students 'cheat' in assessments for all kinds of reasons, but making tasks more engaging can mitigate some of the risk.

Here are some examples:

1. **Computer Science:** Students could be tasked with developing a mobile or web application to solve a real-world problem. They would need to go through the stages of planning, design, coding, testing and deployment, and finally present their application and a report of their process, challenges faced and how they overcame them.
2. **Literature:** Students could create a literary magazine featuring original short stories, poems and essays, along with literary analysis of classic or contemporary works. They would be responsible for the curation, editing, design and publication of the magazine, either in print or digitally.
3. **Music:** Students could be tasked with composing an original musical piece based on a particular theme or historical period. They would then perform the piece, either solo or as part of a group, and submit a reflection on their creative process and the techniques used in their composition.
4. **Product Design and Technology:** Students could identify a common problem and design a product to address it. They would then create a prototype, document the design process, gather feedback, make improvements and present their final design along with a reflection on the iterative design process.

5. **Environmental Science:** Students could conduct a study on a local environmental issue, such as pollution, wildlife habitat destruction or energy consumption. They would collect and analyse data, propose solutions and present their findings to the community or a local governmental body.

Observations

As I mentioned earlier, the vocational sector has a lot to offer when it comes to real-world, non-essay-based assessment tasks. Many of these kinds of tasks are 'GenAI-proof' because they happen away from devices under practical circumstances.

Observations can be conducted in a range of scenarios, including performance tasks, as part of longer projects and during group work. The difference is the student likely knows that the observed period of time is their assessment, and is (hopefully) aware of the explicit criteria.

That can add some pressure to the task, but only the kind of pressure that the student is likely to face in a real-world scenario, and not the false pressure of an examination.

In VET subjects, an assessment tool is a framework for evaluating students' knowledge and skills, comprising assessment context, tasks, evidence-gathering guidelines, performance-quality criteria and administrative requirements. These tools, guided by principles of validity, reliability, flexibility and fairness, ensure that assessments are accurate, consistent, negotiable and equitable.

The design of these tools necessitates industry consultation and testing on a student sample to ensure the evidence collected is valid, sufficient, current and authentic, aligning with the competency units' criteria. This includes the design of assessment tools for observations. Tools like observation checklists, accompanying questions, and instructions for both students and lecturers/observers support this method.

Here are some examples of observation-based tasks across different disciplines:

Mathematics
- *Task:* Solving a series of progressively complex algebraic equations.

- *Checklist:* Correct application of algebraic rules, accurate simplification, correct answer and clear presentation of solution steps.

Science (Physics)
- *Task:* Conducting a physics experiment to measure the acceleration due to gravity.
- *Checklist:* Correct setup of equipment, accurate measurement collection, proper calculation of acceleration, and thorough documentation of the process and results.

Health and Physical Education
- *Task:* Demonstrating a series of gymnastic routines.
- *Checklist:* Correct form and technique, smooth transitions between movements, adherence to safety guidelines and completion of all required routines.

Product Design and Technology (Food)
- *Task:* Preparing a three-course meal adhering to nutritional guidelines.
- *Checklist:* Proper hygiene practices, correct measuring and mixing, adherence to recipe instructions, presentation of the final dishes and nutritional balance.

Digital Technology (Computer Programming)
- *Task:* Coding a simple game using a programming language like Python or Java.
- *Checklist:* Correct syntax, efficient code structure, functionality of the game, debugging and troubleshooting skills, and user-interface design.

Visual essays

The final type is an essay… of a sort. The University of Hertfordshire calls a visual essay 'a critical commentary', which I think is a perfect description of many kinds of essay, including traditional written ones. We want students to be able to give a critical, personal and insightful commentary on their topic, whatever the form.

A visual essay is a curated series of images, either original or significantly processed (including using GenAI), that together provide critical commentary on a specific topic, functioning as a form of argument or discussion. The sequence and layout of images, accompanied by captions or integrated text, guide the 'reading' of the essay. Despite seeming less demanding, creating a visual essay requires effort comparable to traditional academic writing.

A visual essay might be presented as a bound sequence, a series of unbound cards or something like a PowerPoint slideshow, with the design and communication being crucial for its success. Like a traditional essay, it requires thorough research, organisation and referencing, with an annotated bibliography using a referencing system.

The number of images and text should correspond to the effort needed for a written essay of a particular word count, for example, 10–12 images with 500–700 words of text for a 1,500-word essay equivalence. The annotated bibliography should detail the usefulness and application of each source in the visual essay.

Here are some examples:

Historical events

- *Topic:* 'The Evolution of Fashion: A Visual Journey Through the 20th Century.'
- *Description:* This visual essay could depict the evolution of fashion throughout the 20th century, showcasing iconic styles from each decade alongside historical contexts that influenced these fashion trends.

Environmental science

- *Topic:* 'The Impact of Plastic Waste on Marine Life.'
- *Description:* A visual essay displaying the consequences of plastic pollution in oceans and seas, with images showcasing affected marine life, polluted areas and comparisons of clean versus polluted waters.

Social issues

- *Topic:* 'The Faces of Homelessness: A Glimpse into Life on the Streets.'

- *Description:* This essay could present a series of portraits and living conditions of homeless individuals, aiming to humanise and shed light on the issue of homelessness.

Technology
- *Topic:* 'The Rise of Smartphones: Transforming Modern Communication.'
- *Description:* A visual essay illustrating the evolution of smartphones, their impact on communication, social interaction and the juxtaposition of traditional versus digital communication methods.

Health and wellbeing
- *Topic:* 'The Mental Health Impact of Pandemic Lockdowns.'
- *Description:* This essay could visually represent personal narratives, statistics and scenes from daily life during lockdown, highlighting the mental health challenges faced by individuals.

Orals and discussions

I'm basing some of this chapter on a great document from Eliana Elkhoury, PhD (2023), which covers types of oral assessments, their characteristics and examples in academic literature. Elkhoury's document is much broader in scope than this chapter, and I've selected just a few of the possibilities that might apply in various contexts.

Oral assessments are nothing new. Having students deliver presentations or PowerPoints is fairly standard in courses in both K-12 and secondary. Unfortunately, oral tasks often get relegated to being 'tacked on' at the end of a unit as an additional assessment on top of the 'real' written task. But oral assessments can and should occasionally *replace*, not simply add to, other modes of assessment in a unit of work. And it's not all about solo speeches and slide decks.

The caveat over this chapter is that there is no 'one-size-fits-all' approach to assessment. Oral assessments may cause anxiety for some students, or may be inaccessible due to language barriers, non-verbal or selective mutism, or other factors.

Oral presentation

Let's get the most obvious kind of presentation out of the way first. Of course, one way for students to demonstrate their knowledge is through a presentation, solo speech, PowerPoint or similar. This has the advantage of allowing an individual to demonstrate knowledge as opposed to a group, and is also a genuinely useful skill for many knowledge-based jobs.

Of course, students could either perform entirely tech-free, or use a variety of tools to help with oral presentations. If you wanted to incorporate GenAI into an oral presentation, students could:

- Use GenAI text generation like ChatGPT, Bing, Bard or Claude to generate ideas, create scripts, edit, and so on
- Use an app like Gamma to create the slides which accompany the presentation
- Use image generation to create visuals, and add them to a standard format like PowerPoint (which currently has the AI-assisted Designer feature, and will soon have Copilot)
- Use an app like Canva, which includes GenAI features such as text and image generation and AI-assisted design

Again, there's no way to guarantee students are not using GenAI if they are completing part of the task out of class. This includes generating the scripts, but also using audio generation to create convincing versions of their voices for recorded orals. Like I said earlier, if you want it to be totally GenAI free, it has to be a supervised task. Otherwise, accept that GenAI might be used and move on. That logic applies for every assessment type in this series.

Debate and discussion

Debates and discussions have been an effective way of sharing, creating and assessing knowledge since long before our current education system existed. As well as being useful for assessing knowledge, debates and discussions can create healthy competition, strengthen critical and creative thinking skills, build communication skills and contribute to more effective ideas.

Again, you could stage a debate or discussion in class with no technology whatsoever. It could be an informal conversation, a deliberately reflective practice like a yarning circle, semi-structured like a fishbowl, Socratic seminar or fully structured like a formal debate.

If you wanted to deliberately incorporate GenAI into a debate or discussion, you could:

- Use a chatbot as a 'participant' in the debate, bearing in mind all of the potential biases and flaws in current language models
- Use a GenAI-generated text or image prompt as a stimulus
- Apply the Socratic Method directly using a chatbot such as 'Socrates'
- Use GenAI as a tool to record, transcribe, summarise and synthesise points from a discussion, freeing up some of the time needed to assess the content so you can focus on delivery, teamwork, communication skills, and so on

You obviously don't have to assess every conversation that happens in a class, tutor group or online discussion. However, these moments can provide useful insights into how individual students are contributing to the overall knowledge demonstrated through the unit.

Pitch

A pitch is a great way for both individuals and groups to demonstrate their knowledge of a subject: if a student can't successfully pitch an idea, they might need to work on their content knowledge. It's also necessary in a pitch to get to the core of the idea, empathise with your audience and develop strong arguments.

A pitch can be delivered off the cuff, but it's better to plan and prepare. Again, it could be tech-free, or might incorporate GenAI in various ways, including:

- Using GenAI as a mock audience member to test and refine ideas; although a chatbot can't replace a real person when developing an idea, it can be a useful starting point
- Using tools like the ones listed earlier to create compelling pitch decks
- Testing the logic and persuasiveness of an argument against a chatbot
- Using GenAI to write code for prototype apps and web pages, noting that a certain level of coding skill would be required to check for errors or issues

Pitches are great for persuading someone to back a project, product or social enterprise, but can be useful for assessing knowledge, too. Even something as simple as an elevator pitch or Gaddie Pitch can allow a student to succinctly demonstrate what they know, without relying on a written response.

Learning conference

Elkhoury's list of oral assessments includes a reference to a paper from Sindija Franzetti about learning conferences (Franzetti, 2023). In the article, Franzetti writes something which I think most of us can identify with: "Like so many of my colleagues, I resent grading for the labor and energy it takes away from doing the meaningful work of teaching to learn." In response to this resentment towards grading assignments, Franzetti suggests learning conferences: individual conversations with students lasting 20–40 minutes, which included reflection on the course, their participation and the assignment.

Here are some ways that GenAI chatbots can be used as part of the conferencing process:

1. **Pre-class preparation and research:** Students can use a chatbot for researching and gathering information pre-lesson, with a reminder to validate accuracy.
2. **Writing practice and error correction:** A GenAI offers immediate technical feedback on writing, including grammar and structure, allowing students to correct errors and improve without waiting for individualised teacher feedback.
3. **Group discussions and peer feedback:** A chatbot can support group discussions and peer feedback sessions, providing prompts, tracking contributions and acting as a resource for small groups while teachers give 1:1 attention.
4. **Conferencing and personalised feedback:** During conferencing, a GenAI provides additional context, individualised feedback based on unique needs and supports follow-up questions, aiding teachers and addressing diverse student requirements.
5. **Vocabulary expansion, reflection and progress tracking:** A chatbot suggests new vocabulary, guides students in reflection and goal setting, and tracks progress, offering a comprehensive record and contextual examples for ongoing improvement.

Interviews and vivas

Interviews and vivas are traditional methods of oral assessment that allow students to demonstrate their knowledge, communication skills and critical thinking in a structured conversation. These formats can encourage students to think on their feet and provide well-thought-out responses to questions or problems posed by an examiner or panel. Questions can be seen or unseen, and the accessibility needs of students should of course be considered.

If you choose to integrate GenAI in interviews and vivas, several strategies can be employed:

- Students could leverage GenAI for preparing responses to potential questions, honing their articulation skills and refining their arguments.
- Chatbots can serve as practice interviewers, providing an opportunity for students to simulate the interview experience and receive immediate feedback.
- GenAI tools could assist in organising and managing interview schedules, transcribing conversations and highlighting key points for assessment.

Incorporating GenAI doesn't have to undermine the value of interviews and vivas, but could add to the preparation, execution and assessment. It goes without saying by this point that any use of the technology before, during or after an interview should be appropriately acknowledged by both the students and the teacher.

Ungrading

Ungrading is an approach that deviates from traditional grading systems, favouring a more feedback-centric model. Instead of focusing on scores or letter grades, the emphasis shifts towards providing detailed, constructive feedback, encouraging students to reflect on their learning and grow from their experiences. Self-assessment and peer review are encouraged in ungrading methods. Alongside other teacher-led forms of feedback, students gain a better understanding of their own learning, the assessment criteria, and benefit from the diverse perspectives of their peers through reflection and critique.

Ungrading, as the name suggests, steers away from traditional letter and number grades. This could definitely help alleviate the fear and competition often associated with grading, and encourage more of the kinds of collaboration and teamwork we're always *saying* we want in the classroom. One huge issue with our current models of assessment is that they get in the way of genuine interactions like this: it's fine to say "work together", but if the end game is a ranking process (like the senior secondary ATAR in Australia), then there's a contradiction.

Clear and transparent assessment criteria remain pivotal in ungrading. Guidelines and expectations are instrumental for effective assessment and meaningful feedback, irrespective of whether there's a letter or number attached.

Ungrading and GenAI

The de-emphasis of competitive grades and a final number means that ungrading has a lot of potential to help with assessment and GenAI. Emily Pitts Donahoe, Associate Director of Instructional Support at the University of Mississippi, and her students Abi and Trey explored the benefits and challenges of ungrading in the context of GenAI on Pitts Donahoe's substack (Donahoe, 2023). Their story reveals the double-edged sword of GenAI in assessment: something most of us are pretty familiar with by now. On the one hand, GenAI tools like ChatGPT can serve as learning aids, especially in assisting writing skills among students. On the other hand, these very tools can tempt students to circumvent the learning by outsourcing their thinking and writing tasks to AI.

Pitts Donahoe labels an entrenched focus on grades as one of the core underlying issues driving students to engage in academic dishonesty. When the primary aim of education shifts towards attaining higher grades rather than gaining knowledge and honing skills, students are more likely to turn to GenAI for completing their assignments. This grade-centric outlook not only undervalues the learning journey, but also undermines the educational goals. It's in this scenario that ungrading emerges as a potential antidote to the GenAI-induced challenges in assessment.

Pitts Donahoe's classroom experiment with ungrading showed a promising shift in students' approach towards learning. By eschewing points or letter grades and instead providing extensive written feedback with opportunities for revision, the ungrading approach redirected the focus towards learning and improvement. This also led to meaningful dialogues with students about the appropriate use of GenAI in the learning process. When instances of misuse of GenAI arose, they became springboards for discussing how such misuse impeded learning rather than just affecting grades. The shift from a product-centred to a process-centred assessment reinstated the value in the learning process and helped students to engage authentically with the material, without the temptation for misusing GenAI.

Challenges of ungrading

Transitioning from traditional grading systems to an ungrading approach obviously comes with a set of challenges. Here are some of the challenges associated with ungrading:

External pressures and self-evaluation

One of the challenges stems from external pressures, particularly when self-evaluation is a component of ungrading. Given that grades often play a crucial role in admissions to further education and job selections, the pressure on students to achieve high grades remains, even in an ungrading setup.

Not all students are equally equipped to self-evaluate, and there's a concern that some students might undervalue their work, while others might overvalue theirs. However, certain strategies like well-described rubrics can help mitigate potential biases in self-rating.

Misinterpretation and misapplication

The true essence of ungrading can easily be lost if not well understood or well implemented. A significant number of educators who attempt ungrading still rely on rubrics, stated learning outcomes and other traditional grading elements, albeit under different terminologies. This misalignment with the core philosophy of ungrading doesn't change the students' assessment in any meaningful way, nor does it alleviate their fears or competitive pressures associated with grading.

Time-consuming feedback

Providing detailed feedback, which is a cornerstone of ungrading, can be time-consuming, especially in large courses. The process demands a substantial amount of time and effort from educators to ensure meaningful feedback that can guide students towards better understanding and improvement.

Scaling challenges

Scaling the ungrading approach to larger classes or institutions with traditional grading ingrained in their systems poses a significant challenge. The logistical and cultural shift required for ungrading may face resistance or implementation hurdles.

Lack of clear standards

In ungrading, the absence of clear standards or specifications might cause ambiguity for both students and educators. Although some versions of ungrading, like specifications grading, attempt to address this by setting clear standards for each assignment, the broader practice of ungrading might face challenges in defining success and understanding progress.

Educational culture and mindset

The entrenched culture of grading and the mindset associated with it can be significant barriers to the adoption of ungrading. Overcoming these cultural and psychological hurdles requires a concerted effort from educators, administrators, students and the broader educational community.

Where to start with ungrading

Transitioning to an ungrading system isn't going to be easy. You'll meet institutional pushback, resistance to change, and no doubt resistance from students who just want to know that final number or letter. The transition should be about creating a culture of trust, feedback and continuous learning, which can then help in mitigating the potential misuse of GenAI technologies.

1. **Transparency and dialogue:** Establish an open dialogue with students about the benefits and limitations of GenAI through

academic integrity conversations, and why/how/where GenAI should and shouldn't be used in the learning process.
2. **A feedback-rich environment:** Replacing grades with detailed feedback can help in shifting the focus from performance to actual understanding and improvement.
3. **Peer and self-assessment:** Encouraging students to engage in peer reviews and self-assessments can promote a deeper understanding of the learning material and the assessment criteria.
4. **Specifications grading:** Consider specifications grading as a variation, which bundles assessments together. Clear and transparent assessment criteria should also be a part of ungrading, helping to maintain high educational standards while promoting authentic learning.
5. **Professional development for educators:** Professional development for educators for this shift is incredibly important. Training on how to provide effective feedback and how to engage students in self and peer assessments will be crucial for the whole faculty or organisation.

Ungrading can be just another tool in the suite of methods you use to rethink assessment for GenAI. It's been around since before GenAI was on our radars, and there are plenty of studies out there exploring the benefits and challenges in both K-12 and tertiary contexts.

CHAPTER 12
Australian Framework for Generative AI in Schools

In December 2023, the Australian Government published the *Australian Framework for Generative AI in Schools* (Department of Education, 2023). It was informed by a consultative process that began earlier in the year in response to the first wave of hype and fear over ChatGPT's release. The framework draws on advice from academics, teachers, students, industry and professional associations.

The framework is a high-level document and outlines six core principles with 25 guiding statements to help schools navigate GenAI. It doesn't offer much in the way of practical advice, so in this chapter I'm going to make some suggestions aligned to each of the core principles. You can take this advice, along with the subsequent section based on the Victorian ICT Network for Education (VINE) guidelines (Furze, 2023), and put some meat on the bones of the framework.

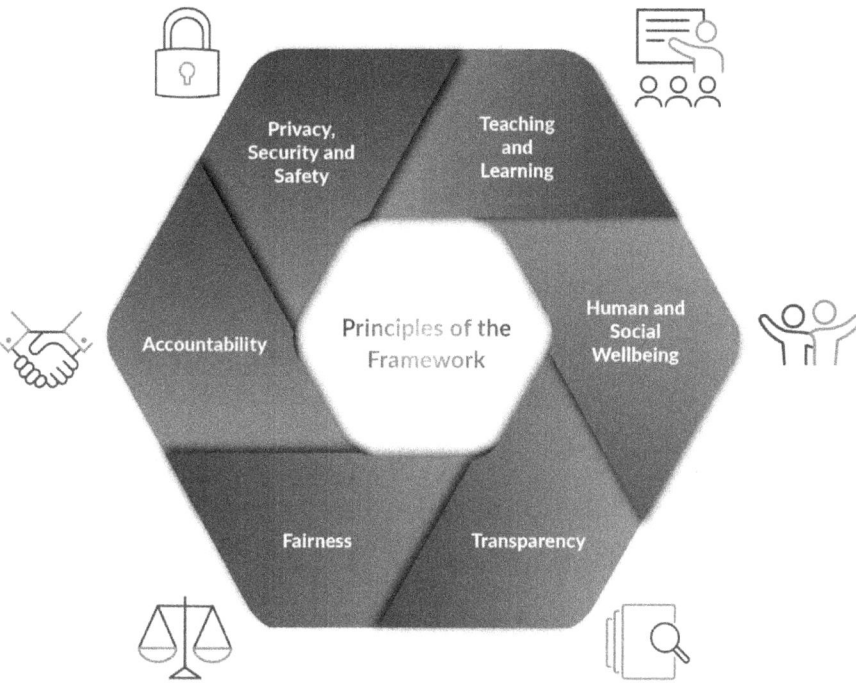

Figure 3: Framework graphic © Commonwealth of Australia, 2023 [CC BY 4.0]

1. Teaching and Learning

Right at the top of the list is the focus on GenAI for Teaching and Learning. This core element is broken down into a positive impact on teaching and learning outcomes, instruction in the technical elements, teacher expertise, critical thinking and academic integrity.

There is further elaboration, which stresses that the positives of GenAI must "clearly outweigh risks or negative implications" and that one way of doing this is through effective instruction, which helps students to avoid harm and use the technology in responsible and accountable ways. The focus on critical thinking reflects concerns that GenAI will lead to an offloading of critical and creative thinking skills, replacing rather than enhancing students' capacity to think for themselves.

A lot has been said about the importance of teaching digital skills, coding, algorithmic thinking and the technical aspects of AI. Some, like Bill Gates, believe that all students need to be taught computer science from an early age.

I think a more nuanced approach would be appropriate – schools don't need to rush into investing in complex AI programs, new subject areas or expert instruction. In fact, many schools in Australia already struggle to deliver just the basics of digital technologies as required by the Australian Curriculum. There are simply not enough digital technologies teachers (or teachers, full stop) to account for new courses in AI.

Instead, my recommendations focus on where GenAI instruction can be worked into existing subject areas, and the kind of support teachers and schools will need to do.

Recommendations

- Determine who is responsible for the implementation of GenAI into the curriculum. This might be a Director of Teaching and Learning or equivalent role, a dedicated subcommittee or team, or another individual appointed specifically for the role. In any case, that person or team should have access to the latest research through academic journals and institutions like the University of South Australia's C3L and Deakin's CRADLE.
- Learning about how GenAI works does not need to be a separate subject – it can be integrated into existing disciplines. GenAI text generation, for example, may fall to the English department, while image generation goes to the Visual Arts and video generation to Media Studies. While interdisciplinary subjects in GenAI seem attractive, the current curriculum, timetables and school structures may make them impractical. Work with what you have now, and consider how subject disciplines might change in the future.
- Invest in professional development in creative and critical thinking skills. There are many opportunities out there which predate this wave of technology, and which focus on teaching and learning practices that prioritise these skills.
- The teaching and learning team should have frank discussions about where GenAI is and is not needed in the curriculum. There will be many occasions where it is preferable to have students working technology-free – that has been the case since long before GenAI was on the agenda. These conversations will overlap with discussions of assessment.

2. Human and Social Wellbeing

This core element advises schools to focus on the potential harms of GenAI and to mitigate these risks by supporting student wellbeing, ensuring a diversity of perspectives, and respecting human rights and the autonomy of individuals.

Of all the elements, this is perhaps the most esoteric and difficult for schools to approach. There are significant ethical concerns with GenAI on a scale which schools can do little to address. Systemic biases are reinforced in the datasets which power these models, and despite the guardrails put in place by developers, may be replicated in the output.

While the framework highlights these issues, there are as yet no concrete suggestions for addressing them. Again, these systems will be implemented in schools before these fundamental issues are addressed on a technological level; in effect, schools will have little choice but to contend with the problems.

Schools can, however, exercise some control over how and where GenAI is implemented, and the conversations had with students, staff and the community.

Recommendations

- Through staff professional development and student instruction, ensure that teachers and students are aware of the inherent biases and potential for discrimination in GenAI systems. These ethical concerns exist at the core of the technology and should be foregrounded in all uses of the technology.
- Consciously analyse GenAI output for potential biases, including through instruction in various subject areas. For example, as part of language analysis in English, students could look for potential bias, discrimination and stereotyping in generated text. Similarly, students could identify and discuss biased representations in image generation.
- Understand that GenAI represents a particular worldview, drawing on a dataset of predominately English language text written by white, Western males. Understand the implications of this, particularly for EAL, culturally diverse and otherwise marginalised students.

- Discuss the implications of bias for assessment practices. Consider how neurodivergent students may be underrepresented in datasets and the implications that might have for students using GenAI to express themselves. Invest in professional development specifically designed with EAL, neurodivergent and otherwise marginalised students in mind.
- Do not implement GenAI into classrooms and assessment practices until clear school policies and guidelines have been written with input from staff, students and the school community.
- Advocate for products and services which have clear approaches to dealing with these ethical concerns. It is highly likely that GenAI will be introduced into schools via existing platforms and services such as Microsoft and Google products, learning management systems (LMSs) and related applications. School and sector leaders interact with these companies at various levels, and as consumers of these products have a right to ask these difficult questions.

3. Transparency

The principles highlight the need for transparency both in how the technologies are used, and how they work. Overlapping with the first two areas, this involves providing clear information about any GenAI tool in use, informed consent and 'explainability'.

Again, there are issues here which schools cannot contend with. The explainability of GenAI systems, for example, is so complex that even the companies who develop the technologies are uncertain of how they actually work. To account for this, the principles highlight that the ability to explain the reasoning behind AI decisions and the impact on individuals should be separated from the 'interpretability' or inner workings of the GenAI model.

In essence, this means that schools must be able to explain how and why GenAI is being used, and the impact on any decision-making in schools, such as assessment practices and curriculum decisions. This may apply to the use of personalised learning chatbots, academic streaming as a result of AI decisions, and so on. There is some crossover in this framework between *Generative*, like ChatGPT, and broader applications of AI, such as predictive algorithms.

Recommendations

- Ensure that all use of GenAI is by informed consent, with the opportunity to opt out. While this may complicate curriculum processes – for example, where GenAI is used in a classroom activity or assessment – it is a necessary process for such an ethically complex technology.
- Informed consent and transparent, plain English statements should be made available to parents and caregivers, possibly as a component of a school GenAI policy.
- A register of GenAI tools and services used by teachers and students should be maintained by an appropriate person or team. There are already thousands of 'AI-powered' apps and services available, and not all are safe or appropriate.
- The register of apps and services should include provisions for teachers to add appropriate software, and should not limit the potential for teachers to explore new technologies or uses.
- Where GenAI is to be used in assessment tasks – by teachers or students – approaches, appropriate apps and services, and exclusions should be made clear in the assessment documentation. For example, if students are permitted to use GenAI in a written task, it should be outlined in the task sheet or instructions. If GenAI is to be used by teachers, for example, in assessment or reporting, this should be made clear in the appropriate documentation or on the LMS.

4. Fairness

This core principle builds on Transparency and the ethical concerns of Human and Social Wellbeing, and requires GenAI to be used in ways which are accessible, fair and respectful. There is potential for GenAI to make certain processes in schools more accessible. For example, natural language processing applications are being developed to help with assistive speech, image recognition for the vision impaired and chatbots for personalised learning.

However, schools should not rush into implementing GenAI for the purposes of personalised learning, differentiation and modification. Given the ethical concerns outlined elsewhere, particularly for the potential discrimination in GenAI, schools should be cautious in how and where GenAI is used.

This principle also covers the important areas of copyright, and cultural and intellectual property.

Recommendations

- In line with other recommendations, keep a register of how and where GenAI is used in teaching and assessment. Ensure that teaching and learning practices are accessible, for example, working with Learning Support staff to identify whether certain students might be excluded from curriculum or assessment practices by implementing GenAI.
- Be cautious of the current technology's capabilities in terms of 'personalised learning'. This is likely to be one of the areas which attracts the most development for GenAI, which also means that it is the most open to companies and developers attempting to take advantage of schools.
- Develop clear and reasonable academic integrity policies, or extend existing policies to incorporate GenAI. Universities are leading the way in developing these policies and guidelines, for example, Deakin University and Monash University. Note that many of these policies do not exclude or penalise the use of GenAI.
- Acknowledge that attempting to 'detect' GenAI is problematic on several levels. There is currently no effective detection software for GenAI. Existing detection software has been demonstrated to discriminate against EAL authors. Detection also places an additional burden on teaching staff and heads of faculty.
- Work with local Indigenous community leaders and identify Indigenous research into the implications of AI for ways of knowing and cultural and traditional practices. Indigenous scholars and organisations are working on understanding the implications of these technologies and should inform school policies and guidelines.
- Respect the copyright of authors, creators and artists. GenAI systems have largely been developed with no regard for intellectual property (IP), and existing models are founded on datasets containing copyrighted materials and IP. Acknowledge this issue in discussions

with staff, students and community, and avoid uses which exacerbate the issue. For example, avoid uses of GenAI in the nature of 'produce writing in the style of...' or image generation which replicates the work of other artists, living or dead.

5. Accountability

The principles recommend that all decision-making ultimately remains in human hands. Sometimes, this is referred to as the 'human in the loop' process. As applied to GenAI, this means that all practices or processes using the technology must have human oversight, and applications and services which automate decision-making should have an ultimate human authority.

Systems must also be operated in ways which are reliable and understood, and monitored to ascertain the impact on student learning. This area will be particularly difficult for schools. At this stage, I don't think there is enough research to clearly identify the impact – positive or negative – of GenAI on learning. As with all digital technologies, schools should avoid the assumption of cause and effect with GenAI and work from the basis that GenAI can improve or detract from learning through how it is used by students and teachers, and not through some inherent effect of the technology itself.

To monitor the impact of GenAI on teaching and learning, schools will need to understand how and where students are using GenAI. There will need to be judgements made about what knowledge and skills benefit from the use of GenAI, and where it would be better for students to learn without the technology.

Recommendations

- As outlined with the first principle, a person or team in the school should have the ultimate responsibility for GenAI-based decision-making in the school. This responsibility should be clearly outlined in the position description of the person or team, and should be supported with appropriate professional development.

- Senior leadership in schools should ensure clear communication with GenAI providers to ensure that they understand the decision-making processes involved. For example, school leaders should attend the forums and panels offered by organisations like Microsoft and Google for education, which provide opportunities to ask questions about reliability and transparency.
- Teachers should be provided with professional development to understand more about the strengths and limitations of GenAI for assessment purposes. For example, while it is possible to enter student work into GenAI like ChatGPT and ask for a summary or feedback, such use may transgress student IP rights and the feedback provided may be impacted by the ethical and bias issues discussed earlier.
- All use of GenAI for assessment and reporting purposes must be clearly understood by staff, students and community.
- Schools should establish guidelines for when and where staff can use GenAI to support assessment and reporting practices. For example, GenAI like ChatGPT can support reporting by turning dot-point notes into more fluent writing, but teachers using the application in this manner should be aware of privacy, IP and related concerns.
- If schools elect to use GenAI in assessment practices, policies should include provisions for students, parents and caregivers to contest any decisions made with GenAI, on the basis that these technologies may be inaccurate.

6. Privacy, Security and Safety

In the schools I have worked with on GenAI policy and guidelines, privacy and security have tended to be among the primary concerns alongside teaching and learning. Most schools have cybersecurity and data-privacy policies, which can be adapted to suit GenAI, and which comply with state and national regulations. However, there are some specific concerns related to GenAI.

The final principle in the framework requires continued compliance with laws and regulations, as well as clear privacy disclosures and protections for students.

Recommendations

- Examine and update existing privacy and data security policies to ensure they are up to date with state and national regulations. As part of a school policy or guidelines for GenAI, include a privacy disclosure statement in plain English for students, parents and caregivers.
- Understand where data entered into GenAI systems is stored, and how it is used. Companies such as OpenAI may use input into GenAI systems for training purposes, meaning data entered by students and teachers becomes part of the dataset. Organisations have varying policies regarding the retention and use of data and should be understood before systems are used in schools.
- Understand the various opt-in and opt-out policies of GenAI apps and services, and the relevant terms and conditions. Include these in the register of technologies suggested above, for example, listing technologies approved for use in the school alongside the terms and conditions for retention of training data.
- Incorporate discussions of GenAI into existing student information on cybersecurity and online privacy. Where external providers are used, for example, for cybersafety talks, enquire as to whether they can incorporate discussions of GenAI.
- Where necessary, de-identify any student data input into GenAI systems. Provide staff professional development into what data can and cannot be entered into GenAI. Never enter personal information about students into GenAI systems without explicit informed consent from students, parents and caregivers, and with a clear understanding of where that data goes and how it is used.
- Only use systems which have a clear and transparent approach to the storage and use of input data. For example, identify systems which do not share data with third-party providers, and which delete user data after 30 days.
- When using systems which interact with personal data, for example, via integration into an LMS or student data system, ensure clarity over how the data is stored and handled.

CHAPTER 13
UNESCO guidelines

Following the 2023 Digital Learning Week in Paris, the United Nations Educational, Scientific and Cultural Organization (UNESCO) published a comprehensive document containing guidelines for GenAI in education and research, and exploring the implications for policy.

The guidelines are linked to the UN Sustainable Development Goals through Goal 4: *Ensure inclusive and equitable quality education and promote lifelong learning opportunities for all*, and reflect the 'Education 2030' agenda of the organisation. As you might expect, there is a focus throughout on human agency, inclusion, equity and diversity. There is also useful advice on the practical and creative implications of GenAI in education which can be applied to the K-12 context.

The guidelines are a useful addition to approaches to GenAI in education but, like all frameworks and guidelines, they need to be contextualised and made as practical as possible if they are to be of any use in the classroom.

The guidelines at a glance

UNESCO's 48-page document covers both the challenges and the opportunities of GenAI for education and research, as well as some broad definitions. The document is structured as follows:

1. What is GenAI and how does it work?
2. Controversies around GenAI and their implications for education
3. Regulating the use of GenAI in education
4. Towards a policy framework for the use of GenAI in education and research
5. Facilitating the creative use of GenAI in education and research
6. GenAI and the future of education and research

In this chapter, I'm going to explore some of the key aspects of these areas and how they can be applied practically in a K-12 context, whether through school policy, guidelines or practical application in the classroom and through teacher professional development.

1. What is GenAI?

The guidelines offer a comprehensive overview of GenAI, focusing on text and image generation, but also touching on video and music. There are some technical details and lists of popular (as of September 2023) applications and services, such as OpenAI's ChatGPT, Google's Bard, Perplexity, DALL·E, Craiyon and Midjourney.

For teachers looking to cut through the 'thousands of AI apps' noise, the apps listed in the guidelines provide a good starting point without going too far. I recommend getting to grips with just one or two GenAI applications, such as ChatGPT and DALL·E, before diving into others. In many cases, current GenAI applications are just interfaces built on top of foundation models like GPT, and therefore do not require different skills.

There is some guidance on prompting, which may be useful to anyone who hasn't yet had the time to explore these technologies. Like I say in the following part of this book, the best way to learn how to prompt GenAI is to get in there and try it out – you'll soon see for yourself the strengths and limitations of different approaches.

I think the most important aspect in this chapter for K-12 educators is the acknowledgement that GenAI spans across different modes: text, visual, audio, video. It is important to recognise that students will be able to use the full multimodal suite of GenAI tools and that, although some like video are currently not great, the pace of development will continue to accelerate.

2. Controversies surrounding GenAI

Part 2 of the UNESCO guidelines focuses on some of the key ethical areas of concern, including those covered in Part 2 of this book. The major 'controversies' in the guidelines include the generation of deepfakes, the 'pollution' of the internet with masses of GenAI content and the potential to worsen the global digital divide. In practical terms, we can educate our students about these concerns and advocate for more transparency and accountability as these systems enter our schools. The ethical concerns with GenAI extend beyond the reach of most individual educators, and can seem too daunting to approach. However, most jurisdictions already have areas of the curriculum designed to approach ethical discussions, and these can be updated to include conversations with students about GenAI.

Schools also have the autonomy to say no to technologies which lack transparency, or which have an over-reliance on student personal data. Over the next few years, we will certainly see an increase in GenAI-powered EdTech, which relies on the datafication of students in the interest of personalised learning. Schools should be cautious which platforms and services they sign up to, and should of course ensure informed consent from students, parents and caregivers.

3. Regulating GenAI in education

Like the bigger-picture ethical concerns on GenAI, regulation of the industry is largely out of the hands of individual teachers and schools. The guidelines provide suggestions for government regulation of GenAI services and providers, and also advice for institutions and individuals as users of the technology.

From a practical perspective, the biggest implications of regulation in the classroom are ensuring that both you and your students understand your rights and responsibilities. Teachers can, for example, help students to navigate the (often deliberately) complex terms and conditions of GenAI applications and services to understand how their data is collected, stored, used and shared. Honestly, *no one* reads terms and conditions – and that's exactly how we got ourselves into such a mess with social media. But this doesn't have to be a boring exercise in reading the small print. Group annotation tools, threads pointing out the absurdity of some terms and conditions, and getting students to write their own 'ethical' terms and conditions can lighten the discussion.

In Australia, the eSafety Commissioner has recently released a position statement on GenAI, which includes suggestions to industry for a 'safety by design' approach. It might not seem like the most flashy or amazing use of GenAI in the classroom, but it is important to discuss with students. The eSafety Commissioner guidance, for example, offers advice on what to do if you are a victim of GenAI-related cyberbullying or abuse, such as explicit deepfakes.

Regulation has been slow to catch up with the developments in GenAI in the past 18 months, but it is catching up. Educators will of course need to make sure that any use of the technology in the classroom is in line with local laws and regulations.

4. GenAI policy in education

The approach to policy in the UNESCO guidelines matches what we've seen here in Australia through the Australian Framework for Generative AI in Schools (see page 70). The policy advice focuses on: inclusion, equity and diversity; human agency; monitoring and evaluation; the development of AI competencies for learners; capacity building for teachers; plurality of expressions and perspectives; local models; and long-term implications.

Again, some of this is beyond the scope of individual schools and teachers. However, the 'AI competencies' will be interesting to keep an eye out for, and UNESCO plans to release its own draft competencies in 2024.

Schools should also be considering how they will provision teacher professional development. Teachers will need support in using the tools, understanding how students might use the tools, academic integrity and assessment practices, and GenAI ethics and appropriate use. Plenty of this professional development is already out there, and it is a case of curating and finding appropriate resources. I was involved in providing some 'Critical Friend' advice for ACARA as it produced the AI Curriculum Connections resources (ACARA, 2023), and it provides a great starting point for definitions, curriculum links for Mathematics and Digital Technologies, the general capabilities and the cross-curriculum priorities.

Personally, one of the reasons I think schools benefit from a clear GenAI policy or guidelines is that they make transparent the expectations for staff professional development. If a school commits to implementing, monitoring and evaluating GenAI, then it must also commit to ensuring sufficient training for the teachers and staff.

5. Creative use of GenAI in education

As I mentioned earlier, there have been some criticisms of the UNESCO guidelines due to the focus on policy, regulation and the ethical concerns of GenAI. Part 5 of the guidelines, however, provides some examples of "potential but unproven uses" of the technology.

We're already seeing a lot of hype over the 'transformational potential' of GenAI, or the ways in which it will 'revolutionise education'. Given the frequent disappointments in the past of EdTech, and the ever-growing digital divide in Australia and globally, I prefer UNESCO's slightly more conservative approach.

There are, undoubtedly, creative applications of these technologies in education. I personally use text, image and audio generation as part of my consulting business and my writing, and I'm sure that I'll use video generation when the technology improves. I've also used GenAI features like ChatGPT's Advanced Data Analysis (formerly code interpreter) to create programs in python and HTML that I would struggle to make myself.

The UNESCO guidelines suggest "human centred and pedagogically appropriate interactions" (UNESCO, 2023, p.23) as an approach to using GenAI; essentially, make sure that GenAI doesn't replace human critical and creative thinking, and don't use it just for the sake of it. I think that's sound advice. We don't need to see any more uncanny valley 'historical talking heads' with AI voiceovers. Instead, we should be looking for occasions where GenAI supports and augments useful teaching strategies.

In terms of personalised learning, schools should be cautious of GenAI. We know that these systems present a normalised, culturally US-centric and non-diverse worldview. Technologies offering personalised learning made inadvertently further marginalise some students. As an example, I'm yet to find any large language model which can accurately represent an autistic worldview beyond outdated and stereotypical paradigms, which centre on the pathologising of autistic traits, such as 'fixing' eye contact and other social skills. Contemporary research based on lived experience needs to be worked into any GenAI personalisation services before they can be used effectively.

It's worth digging in to pages 30–35 of the guidelines for some examples of potential uses, as well as some of the caveats and risks associated with them. These include:

- GenAI as a research advisor
- GenAI literature reviewer
- Curriculum co-designer

- Chatbot teaching assistant
- 1:1 GenAI coach or tutor
- 'Socratic challenger'
- Project-based learning advisor
- Learning difficulty diagnostic/accessibility tool

6. GenAI and the future of education and research

The brief final section of the UNESCO guidelines includes discussion of the 'uncharted territory' of the future of GenAI. This section revisits the ethical concerns and emphasises the need to promote equitable access, mitigate bias and respect intellectual property. The final section of the guidelines also discusses the need for critical and creative thinking skills and ways we might avoid offloading too many of our skills (or our students') onto AI.

CHAPTER 14
Writing school guidelines

This part of the book provides an overview of the approach I've taken to helping schools write GenAI guidelines, which includes updating academic integrity policies and assessment practices. GenAI guidelines have to go beyond assessment and include privacy and safety concerns, and require input from the school community.

This chapter is based in part on work I completed in 2023 with the Victorian ICT Network for Education (VINE). We produced a comprehensive set of guidelines based on the then-draft Australian Framework for Generative AI in Education. VINE very kindly made the guidelines open access, and you can find them here on the VINE website: vine.vic.edu.au

Conducting a policy audit

Before getting into the guidelines, conduct a policy audit. You are likely to find that your school or institution already has documents which can be easily updated rather than beginning from scratch. Here are the documents I recommend looking for:

- Academic integrity/honesty policy
- Assessment policy/guidelines
- Senior school assessment guidelines based on VCAA advice
- Cyber/digital user agreements (student and/or parent/caregiver)
- Cybersafety/digital consent/guidelines arising from the Australian Resilience, Rights and Respectful Relationships program or similar
- Advice on any AI-related software licences in school (for example, Microsoft 365, Adobe Creative Cloud, Google Workspace for Education or your LMS)
- Any other policies or guidelines which may be related to GenAI

Questions to frame your discussion

Begin the work of updating or creating GenAI guidelines by using the following questions in a school or organisational leadership meeting. These questions might also help to identify gaps in the policies you found earlier:

1. What is the overall stance on AI usage in secondary education? Is there a unified view on this issue among staff, students and parents/caregivers, or are there conflicting perspectives that need to be reconciled? How do you know?
2. How does the organisation define 'generative AI'? Does it include only text-generation tools like ChatGPT or is it extended to include image, audio and video generation?
3. How will the organisation approach the ethical use of AI, including the issue of academic integrity? How will the organisation ensure that students understand and abide by these ethical guidelines?
4. What policies will the organisation implement to ensure student data privacy when using AI tools? How will these policies align with the guidelines proposed by the education department, which emphasise safeguarding personal information?
5. How will the organisation educate students and staff about the potential privacy and accuracy issues associated with AI use?
6. To what extent will AI tools be incorporated into assessment practices? At what levels of the AI Assessment Scale will AI usage be permitted and in which situations would it be inappropriate or prohibited?
7. How will the organisation manage the use of AI in brainstorming, ideas generation, outlining and notes, feedback and editing, and full AI generation? How will these different levels of AI integration be monitored and evaluated?
8. How will AI-generated content be cited and acknowledged in student work to maintain academic integrity? What penalties will apply for failing to appropriately cite AI-generated content?
9. How will the organisation ensure that AI is used as a tool to enhance student learning?
10. How will the organisation communicate its AI policies and guidelines to students, parents/caregivers, the community and staff? What mechanisms will be in place for revising and updating these policies as AI technologies and their usage evolve?

11. How will the organisation integrate AI tools into task design and assessment methods? How will it ensure that these tasks allow students to demonstrate their unique achievements and critical thinking skills?
12. How will the organisation support staff in acquiring the necessary skills and knowledge to effectively use AI tools in teaching and assessment practices?
13. How will the organisation measure the impact of AI on teaching and learning outcomes? What mechanisms will be put in place for continuous evaluation and improvement of AI usage in the school?
14. How will the organisation manage any potential challenges or conflicts that may arise from integrating AI into teaching and assessment practices?

1. Teaching and learning

In creating guidelines for the use of GenAI in educational settings, whether in schools or tertiary institutions, it's important to approach the subject with a nuanced understanding of the complexities and evolving nature of technology and its integration into teaching and learning environments. Remember that technology doesn't *automatically* improve (or harm) pedagogy.

Academic integrity and assessment

Upholding academic integrity is fundamental across all disciplines. Educators should clearly communicate to students the importance of trust, honesty and respect in academic endeavours, irrespective of the use of GenAI. This includes a commitment to completing work to the best of one's ability, proper acknowledgment of sources and contributions from others, including GenAI tools, and maintaining transparency in academic work. Students facing challenges should feel encouraged to seek support or extensions. Luckily, none of this is new; it's likely that your existing academic honesty policies won't need updating much.

Assessment practices might need to adapt to accommodate GenAI, recognising that GenAI's detection is not always reliable. As discussed earlier in the AI Assessment Scale chapter, educators should consider a spectrum of GenAI use in assessments, ranging from prohibiting GenAI to using it for brainstorming, outlining, editing or even completing entire tasks. Schools might form working groups to explore GenAI's impact on assessments, test GenAI tools against current assessments and clearly articulate the role of GenAI in various assessment stages.

Professional learning

Given the rapid development of GenAI technologies, educational institutions should commit to regular, accessible professional learning to ensure staff understand the ethical and practical aspects of GenAI. Curating GenAI-related resources, conducting seminars and encouraging resource sharing among staff are strategies that can support educators in this evolving landscape.

2. Privacy and security

Existing policies and legal frameworks will be very useful in helping to create GenAI guidelines. Many of the potentially harmful uses of GenAI are already covered by existing laws, and it's highly likely that your organisation will have existing policies concerning things like data breaches and student data privacy.

Understanding GenAI privacy

Educational organisations need to recognise the potential risks to privacy posed by GenAI tools. There should never be any entry of personal or identifying information into any GenAI application, and staff and students should be educated about the risks associated with sharing personal data with GenAI services, and understanding the implications for privacy, such as the potential creation of deepfakes or malicious content.

Schools should incorporate GenAI discussions into existing cybersafety talks, maintain a clear register of GenAI apps and services, particularly regarding their terms and conditions, and ensure that staff avoid using personal data in GenAI applications for tasks like report writing or creating individualised learning plans.

Secure use of GenAI apps and services

The terms and conditions of GenAI apps and services need to be clearly understood by all users, including students and teachers. Make sure all staff are also aware of the processes for handling data breaches, since even the accidental input of personal information into some GenAI systems might constitute a reportable breach.

Schools can enhance security by consulting with IT administration on data handling, selecting trusted apps with transparent terms and limiting the use of unknown third-party applications through a vetting process. This not only aligns with existing digital policies, but also promotes a safer GenAI environment.

GenAI and student safety

The personal safety and rights of students must be the highest concern. GenAI technologies can be misused to create illegal or abusive content, including deepfakes. Educating staff and students about reporting processes for GenAI-related abuse, incorporating discussions on GenAI abuse in digital safety talks, and enforcing school policies and legal measures against breaches, are critical.

Practical strategies include using resources from the eSafety Commissioner for education, familiarising staff with relevant laws concerning explicit content, and engaging the community, including parents and caregivers, in understanding and participating in reporting processes for GenAI-related abuse.

3. Fairness, accessibility and equity

In addressing fairness, accessibility and equity in the context of GenAI within educational environments, it is important to ensure that these technologies are implemented in a manner that is inclusive and ethically sound. This includes careful selection and usage of GenAI apps and services, as well as a keen awareness of the ethical concerns, particularly regarding biases inherent in current GenAI technologies.

Addressing bias and marginalisation in GenAI

GenAI technologies often reflect biased worldviews due to the nature of their training datasets. For instance, datasets used by LLMs may be skewed towards English language data predominantly generated by certain demographics, leading to biases and potentially harmful outputs. Educational institutions should acknowledge these biases and educate their community about them. The use of GenAI in assessment or feedback should be monitored for bias, and GenAI tools should be selected based on their efforts to mitigate discriminatory outputs.

Fair and transparent use of GenAI

Fairness and transparency are vital when GenAI is used by teachers or students. This involves disclosing the use of GenAI in resource creation, assessments and communications to ensure alignment with academic integrity and ethical standards. To implement this, schools could engage with parents and caregivers to determine acceptable uses of GenAI, remind staff regularly about the need for disclosure, and use approaches to ensure communications are accurate and authentic.

Accessibility and GenAI for personalised learning

While GenAI has potential in enhancing accessibility and personalised learning, its effectiveness and appropriateness, especially for students with disabilities or neurodevelopmental disorders, remain uncertain. Schools must be cautious in using GenAI for creating individualised learning resources, recognising the limitations and biases of current GenAI technologies.

I'll talk more about this in Part 4 when I discuss GenAI prompts for personalising resources, lesson plans and individual learning.

CHAPTER 15
Example academic integrity policy

Having said in the previous chapter that you're likely to have an academic integrity policy that won't need much updating, it's still worth looking at a fully developed policy to compare what you already have. Academic integrity is without a doubt the biggest concern around GenAI in education (whether that should be the case or not).

Here is the complete academic integrity policy adapted from the VINE guidelines:

i. **Introduction**
   a. The organisation endorses this Policy from DATE.

ii. **Purpose**
   a. The purpose of this document is to set forth the tenets and responsibilities critical for safeguarding academic integrity standards within the organisation's community.

iii. **Applicability**
   a. This guideline pertains to all organisation students and to anyone else who submits academic work for evaluation at our institution.
   b. For senior academic undertakings (for example, Victorian Certificate of Education, Vocational Education and Training, and Vocational Major), students must conform to this Policy alongside any associated conduct standards.

c. Faculty and administrative staff are also bound to this Policy, ensuring they not only embody, but also enforce and uphold these academic integrity standards.

iv. **Understanding academic integrity**

a. At its core, academic integrity is anchored in principles of trust, honesty, respect and fairness, creating a respectful educational environment for all stakeholders.

b. Such integrity guarantees that educational outcomes reflect genuine understanding and are intrinsically tied to an ethos of ethical professionalism.

v. **GenAI and academic integrity**

a. Recognising the advent of digital tools like GenAI, the organisation establishes the following:

i. GenAI in academic work: Be it for classwork, homework or assessments, any task should be the authentic creation of the student, whether GenAI is used or not.

ii. GenAI modes: Understand that GenAI has various modes, including text, audio and visual content generation. All of these should be approached with the same standards of integrity.

iii. Crediting GenAI: If any form of GenAI, be it text, visual or audio, contributes to one's task, it is imperative to acknowledge the specific tools or methods utilised.

vi. **Key principles in upholding integrity**

a. Transparency and authenticity: Commit to being open about all sources and contributions. Honesty should be paramount in every academic endeavour.

b. Seeking assistance: If challenges arise, students should not hesitate to consult relevant educators for guidance, additional resources or extensions.

vii. **Violations of academic integrity**

a. Potential breaches encompass:

i. Plagiarism: The act of borrowing from others' works without due credit.

ii. Outsourcing: Entrusting academic tasks to third parties or entirely to GenAI tools without attribution.
iii. Collusion: Working in tandem with peers to present shared work as individually crafted.
iv. Misrepresentation: Deliberately distorting or falsifying data, findings or information.
v. Academic dishonesty: Gaining an undue edge through deceptive documents or actions.

viii. Roles and responsibilities
    a. Students' duties:
        i. Engage diligently with academic resources.
        ii. Grasp and adhere to the organisation's expectations around integrity.
        iii. Practice and champion integrity in academic and interpersonal activities.
    b. Educators' obligations:
        i. Model integrity in professional conduct.
        ii. Design assignments that inherently reduce chances of integrity violations.
        iii. Educate, support and guide students in understanding and upholding integrity.
    c. Institutional responsibilities:
        i. Equip educators to perform their roles effectively in this regard.
        ii. Investigate, address and adjudicate on reported breaches of integrity.
        iii. Ensure all external collaborations and partnerships are in alignment with our integrity ethos.

ix. Policy revision
    a. Periodically, the organisation's governing board will evaluate this Policy for its ongoing relevance, ensuring it continuously promotes the essence of academic integrity.

Note that this policy would be used in conjunction with the AI Assessment Scale from earlier to ensure students have clarity over when and how AI can be used in a task. It assumes that students *want* to be honest and do the right thing, but we need to clearly articulate what that looks like.

The most important aspect of academic integrity is ensuring both students and staff are clear on what is and is not appropriate.

CHAPTER 16
Do you need this application or platform?

I work with many schools, tertiary providers and organisations trying to navigate AI policy and guidelines like those suggested earlier. Some education providers are using the Australian Framework for Generative AI in Secondary Schools as a guideline. Others are using UNESCO materials or drawing on their own research. Most have only just started the process and are looking for clear advice.

One huge issue is the speed of development of GenAI, especially chatbot technologies like ChatGPT and Bing, image generation like DALL·E and Adobe Firefly, and even video, audio and code generation. Trying to keep up with each new app and feature is impossible, and sometimes it's better to hold off than rush in to poorly designed or inappropriate apps and services. A few weeks prior to starting this book, OpenAI released another update which will knock out many AI start-ups, including in EdTech. Sometimes, it really is more appropriate to wait.

Recently, I learned that there's a term for this: the Wait Calculation. The Wait Calculation suggests that, with technology advances, sometimes it's better to wait a while for a more advanced technology to come along than to rush in. The example given is space travel: if you were to set off now with current technology, you'll be passed in a few decades by someone who set off later with better tech. Sometimes, the reward of being a first mover is greater than the risk of being outdone in the long term. At other times, it's better to stay on planet Earth and wait for the technology to mature. The same is true with AI.

The Need/Potential Matrix

The Need/Potential Matrix is a tool based on an Eisenhower matrix – you might have seen it for deciding whether things are important, urgent or some combination.

In this context, it's a useful tool for deciding whether an AI technology, app or system is worth diving into now or waiting a while (or not worth it at all). It's also focused on the needs of your organisation, whether that's K-12, tertiary or outside of education. It asks: Do we need this technology? Do we need it right now? What will happen to it in the future?

Here's what the matrix looks like:

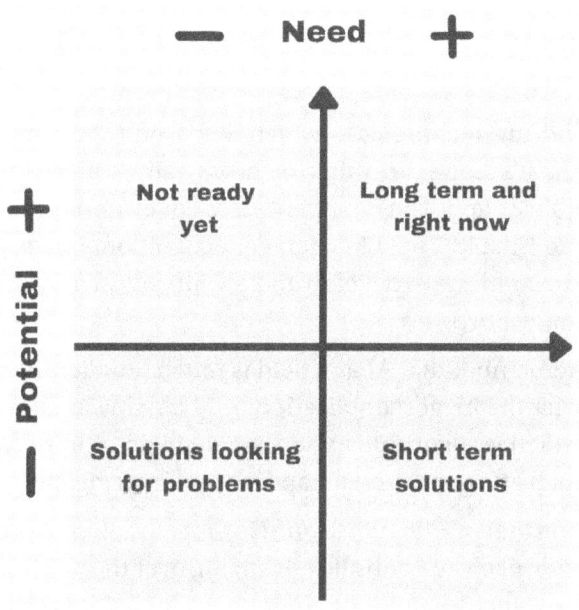

Figure 4: The Need/Potential Matrix

Examples of the Need/Potential Matrix in action

Quadrant 1: Low immediate need and high future potential

Q1 technologies include anything on the mid-far horizon, but which offer huge potential. It's a 'watch and wait' quadrant that might include technologies like quantum computing, brain-computer interfaces, autonomous vehicles and advanced robotics.

The chances of bringing these technologies into classrooms directly is slim, but it's likely that some students will encounter these fields in the future, and you could certainly partner with universities and industry to explore what's possible.

Quadrant 2: High immediate need and high future potential

In Q2 you'll find the technologies which are useful *right now* and have future potential. It's better to think of fields rather than specific apps, knowing how quickly apps can be superseded. For example, the technology behind apps like ChatGPT – LLMs, image recognition, image generation, etc – are going to continue to develop and are already at a stage where they are useful for many purposes.

It also pays to remember that AI as a field is much broader than *generative* AI, and that by far the biggest application of AI already in education is not GenAI, but predictive algorithms and data analytics. These technologies need just as much attention, understanding and interrogation.

I'm of the opinion that *multimodal* GenAI is the technology worth following here, as it is highly likely to continue advancing over the next few years and will also drive advances in a lot of other areas, including augmented and virtual reality. Multimodal GenAI, including image generation/recognition, code, internet browsing, video, audio and of course text generation, is also right here and right now, and has many immediate applications.

Quadrant 3: Low immediate need and low future potential

These are toys and distractions – technologies which might be driven by hype or marketing, but which don't have a lot of substance. For all kinds of reasons, I feel that most 'chatbots' and web applications built on top of GPT (such as 'teacher lesson planning AI assistants' and the like) fall into this category.

These technologies don't address a real current need (I understand it's attractive to generate bulk lesson plans, but what teachers really need is more time and fewer administrative overheads to create their own resources), and they don't have longevity. Most are quickly superseded, and the industry is too unpredictable to invest time and money into things that might disappear in a month or two.

Quadrant 4: High immediate need and low future potential

These are apps and services which are worth paying attention to, but not building an entire system around. *Some* chatbots might fall into this category, though I'd suggest they'd have to be solidly built and backed by some serious safety features (which generally means serious money, given how much of a target these systems are for attacks).

ChatGPT itself might fall into this category. It has great potential for immediate use, but OpenAI is yet to create a truly successful and sustainable business model, and a company like Microsoft might ultimately absorb it or replace it. That doesn't mean it's not worth learning how to use ChatGPT *right now*, though, since the skills learned on that one platform are transferable to other GenAI applications and systems.

Questions for decision-making

To make the matrix even more useful, you can use the following questions to help judge the Need and Potential of the technology or application under review. Obviously, there is an element of human judgement here and you also need some insights into the technology and its future. You'll also need a solid understanding of the problems you're trying to solve.

One way to use these is to score each question out of 5, and then use the total score to determine (at your discretion) whether it falls into the 'high' or 'low' range for Need and Potential.

- Low: 0–23
- Mid: 24–37
- High: 38–50

Questions based on Need (each out of 5)

1. Does this technology directly address a current challenge in our institution?
2. Is there a demand from stakeholders (students, staff, parents/caregivers) for this kind of solution?
3. How does this technology align with our current curriculum or teaching methodologies?
4. Can the technology be easily integrated with our existing infrastructure?
5. Does this tool offer a solution that is significantly better than our current methods or tools?
6. Will this technology reduce workload or administrative burdens for staff?
7. Is the learning curve for this technology manageable for our staff and students?
8. Can the tool be implemented without significant disruption to current processes?
9. Does the technology provide any immediate cost savings or efficiencies?
10. Is there data or evidence supporting the tool's effectiveness in similar educational settings?

Questions based on Potential (each out of 5)

1. How scalable is this technology as our institution grows or evolves?
2. Is there a clear roadmap for the technology's future development?
3. What are the chances this technology will become obsolete in the next five to 10 years?
4. Can this tool be adapted or customised to meet future challenges or changes in curriculum?
5. Is there potential for this technology to foster new ways of teaching or learning that we haven't considered?
6. Does this technology have a supportive community or ecosystem for continuous learning and sharing?
7. Are there any emerging trends in education that this technology is poised to capitalise on?
8. How does the technology position our institution in terms of being a leader in innovation?

9. Are there opportunities for collaboration or partnerships because of this technology?
10. Is there potential for the tool to offer long-term cost savings or become more cost-effective over time?

For an example of a 'scored' process using ChatGPT as the technology, you can check out the original post on my blog about the Need/Potential Matrix here: leonfurze.com/2023/11/15/ai-policy-toolkit-the-need-potential-matrix.

PART 4
Practical strategies for GenAI

CHAPTER 17
Planning

Using GenAI to assist with lesson planning, the creation of resources, and the development of scope and sequence is almost certainly where you will get the most use out of the technology. We know that planning is incredibly important for creating structured, meaningful courses that address students' needs. Unfortunately, after administration, face-to-face time, meetings, extracurricular duties and other interruptions, we often find that planning gets pushed aside and left to occasional staff days.

In fact, planning is such an obvious area for applying GenAI that hundreds of apps and services have sprung up since November 2022 that use the technology to create lesson plans and classroom resources. Unfortunately, there's a problem with these kinds of technology: they are usually sold as 'reducing teacher workload', but in fact they *replace* core parts of the educator's role. They are also typically built on top of LLMs like OpenAI's GPT and offer little more than a 'wrapper' around the core model. This means that anything you can do in a *lesson planning AI app*, you could probably do yourself directly through an application like ChatGPT, Claude or Bing.

As I've discussed elsewhere in this book, we don't want to offload the important work of planning lessons and creating resources onto GenAI. We want to use the technology to support our own expertise and professionalism.

Prompts for planning

The following prompts cover a range of approaches for using GenAI for creating lesson plans, resources, units of work, and so on. Throughout this part of the book, more complex prompts are discussed in detail to show exactly why they work. Some prompts require internet-connected applications like Microsoft's Bing Chat. Occasionally, a prompt uses a feature only available in the paid version of applications like ChatGPT Plus, though I have avoided these where possible. As always, the applications and models are likely to come and go, so find models that work for you, but focus on the core skills of writing clear, consistent prompts.

Lesson on <topic> should meet the following outcomes: <copy/paste outcomes from curriculum documents>. Suggest learning outcomes for an introductory lesson which covers <content>

This prompt will give you learning outcomes, but should not create the entire lesson plan. You can use this as a starting point or to quickly align content to curriculum outcomes.

This first prompt introduces a few important concepts you will see throughout this part of the book:

- The topic and content are decided by the teacher. You can ignore the <> throughout: I use them to indicate where additional material might be added.
- I use a copy/paste of outcomes from curriculum materials (for example, ACARA, your state curriculum, the common core). This anchors the prompt and makes it much more specific to your required content.
- Wherever you see <copy/paste...> you could also use a link to a website in a browser-enabled application like Microsoft Bing Chat.

How can technology be used to enhance the learning experiences in this lesson on <topic>? <copy/paste lesson plan>. Identify three specific ways technology can be integrated into the lesson to support student understanding and engagement.

This prompt takes an already developed lesson plan and reviews it to suggest ways to integrate technology. You could make this even more specific by including examples of technology use from curriculum documentation in the prompt, or by beginning with a prompt like **browse online for best practice in using technology to support student engagement.**

Role play: You are a teacher in our <subject> faculty. We are currently in a meeting to discuss a unit of work on <topic> for Year <year level> students. You are knowledgeable, but highly critical and a little cynical. Your role is to critique and question the unit plan, and we will type our responses. Do not provide our responses, only your responses. Here is the unit plan: <copy/paste unit plan>

There's a lot going on in this prompt, so let's break it down:

- Role play: Telling the model that you are 'role playing' or that it has a specific persona is a very useful technique that can be applied in many situations. Use a 'role play' prompt when you want the model to respond from a very specific perspective.
- Do not attempt to have a model role play as a real person – living or dead. There is no LLM capable of modelling the full complexity of a human, and it will result in a two-dimensional response.
- Instead, give the model broad character descriptions and dispositions. In this case: 'teacher', 'knowledgeable', 'highly critical' and 'a little cynical'.
- Provide clear instructions like: "Your role is to critique and question the unit plan…"
- The final instruction, "Do not provide our responses…", is there because LLMs often continue both sides of the discussion, and you don't necessarily want it to tell you what you think.

This prompt will most likely result in a list of 10 critical questions based on the unit you provide. It is a great way of getting a different perspective on a unit, particularly if you don't have much time to meet as a faculty or if you are a 'faculty of one' for your subject.

Based on the curriculum standard <copy/paste specific curriculum standard> and the attached resource <upload, copy/paste or link to resource>, generate a set of questions and answers that address these standards for <year level/subject>. Include a brief explanation of how each resource aligns with the curriculum standard.

This prompt demonstrates how to 'DIY' those lesson-planning apps I mentioned at the start of this chapter. There are many ways to provide context for a model, including uploading files directly, copy/pasting as we have been doing already or linking to a resource in a browser-enabled model.

Increasingly, most applications like ChatGPT, Bing, Bard and Claude feature the ability to upload PDFs, Word documents, PowerPoints and so on to use as contextual material. Many models can also use image recognition, which you'll see in the next prompt.

Using the attached notes, create an outline for a unit of work lasting for eight weeks on the topic of <topic> for <year level/subject>. <Attach image of notes>

You can attach a photo of notes on a whiteboard, handwritten notes from a notepad or a collection of sticky notes, and the LLM can use image recognition to take the notes and turn them into a draft document. Image recognition can be hit or miss, but the ability continues to improve and generally works well with legible handwriting.

Generate a list of resources and materials we will need during this unit of work: <copy/paste unit of work>

This simple prompt provides a quick way to review a unit of work and identify resources. You could be even more specific with the prompt and ask for physical resources, electronic resources, supporting references, useful websites (in a browsing-enabled model), and so on.

Write a <blog post/article/exemplar paragraph/short analytical piece, etc...> on the topic of <topic> for <year level/subject>. The tone and style should be <tone/style notes>. It should have the following <features/evidence>

This is an example of a versatile prompt for creating written resources, such as persuasive texts, analytical pieces, short articles, blog posts, etc. It requires quite a lot of explicit instructions over the form, tone and style, but can be adapted to suit a wide range of contexts. For example, an English teacher could use the prompt to create lesson resources for teaching paragraphing. A Science teacher might use a prompt like this to create short case studies or discussions. A Humanities teacher might create a short article or essay for discussion in class.

Outline an experiment for <topic>. Use code interpreter to model the experiment and produce some mock data, and then graph the outcome of the experiment. Give a detailed explanation of the entire experiment.

This prompt relies on code interpreter (which ChatGPT also calls 'data analysis'), which at the time of writing is a paid feature of ChatGPT Plus. It allows the model to both write and execute code, meaning that it can use programming languages like python to handle complex mathematics. This prompt could be used, for example, to create a physics experiment with accompanying explanation and graphs to use as a lesson resource. Code interpreter has many more applications (I used it in the creation of this book to write a small piece of software – see page xi for more details).

Reflect and extend

These prompts have been designed to introduce some core concepts, such as providing contextual information like curriculum outcomes, but also to demonstrate that there is no single 'magic formula' for prompting. Each chapter in this part of the book includes reflections and extensions for the prompts in that chapter.

Here are some reflections for using prompts for *planning*:

- How can you use GenAI to support, but not offload, the work of lesson planning?
- In what other scenarios could you imagine a 'role play' prompt being useful?
- How could *planning* prompts be used as part of a collaborative curriculum development process, such as working in faculty or year-level teams?

Throughout this book the advice is to *get in there and experiment* to find out which models and approaches you prefer. One aspect of that experimentation is looking for ways to extend the prompts in each chapter. Here are some ways you could extend these prompts:

- Combine prompts in a single chat thread to keep developing the ideas. For example, begin with the first prompt on lesson outcomes, and then move on to creating a fully developed lesson plan with activities. Use that as the basis to generate resources that leverage websites, existing materials uploaded as PDFs, and so on.

- Extending the 'role play' idea, continue the dialogue once the model generates the initial questions by responding with your answers and prompting for further feedback.
- Experiment with more advanced features such as image recognition and code interpreter. We will come across these features again in future chapters, but if you have access to these features it is good to start experimenting with them early.

CHAPTER 18
Refreshing

As well as creating new resources, educators spend a lot of time refreshing and updating old materials. This might be because the school or organisation switches to a new teaching and learning framework, or because of curriculum changes. Alternatively, it could just be because the materials are getting a bit tired. A lot of the time we end up throwing out perfectly good materials because it's quicker to start over.

GenAI can be used to quickly update materials, align with new curriculum outcomes or take some of the work out of moving resources from one form or template to another. It also means that we're not reinventing the wheel and can save a lot of time in curriculum planning and resourcing.

Prompts for refreshing

The prompts in this chapter are designed to help with the process of updating old resources. There are ways to update both digital and hard-copy materials, and prompts which help to analyse existing lesson plans, units and resources, and suggest improvements.

<copy/paste a unit of work into the LLM>. Use this unit of work as the basis for a new unit outline. Keep the same core topics, but suggest more engaging activities and formative assessment methods. Focus particularly on adding group work and opportunities for students to engage in practical activities.

This prompt offers a way to quickly review and update an existing unit of work. Of course, you'll need to exercise your own judgement over what the model decides is 'engaging', since you know your students better than the technology. GenAI models generally do a good job of suggesting formative assessment methods and 'hurdle' tasks, but again your professional expertise is always needed for the final work.

This is an example of our school teaching and learning framework: <copy/paste teaching and learning framework>. We also use the following approach for designing rubrics: <copy/paste rubric design framework>. Update this existing rubric to better reflect our teaching and learning framework and school approach to building rubrics: <copy/paste old rubric>

In this prompt, an old rubric is updated to a new version by comparing it to new teaching and learning methods. Your teaching and learning framework, pedagogical approach, institutional policies, and so on can all be used to guide the model's output. You might also have a school- or institution-wide policy for assessment, which determines the format of your rubrics, such as whether you use developmental rubrics, how many criteria are required, and so on. This prompt will produce a new rubric based on those conditions.

Role play: You are a student in a <subject> class. Your teacher has just announced that the class will be refreshing an existing unit on <topic>. Your role is to provide feedback on the current unit and suggest changes you would like to see in the refreshed unit. Here is the existing unit plan: <copy/paste unit plan>

Like the role play prompt in the previous chapter, this prompt gives explicit instructions of the role and purpose of the model – in this case, a student reviewing a unit of work. Of course, this doesn't replace the need for getting *actual* student feedback and collaboration on unit design, but it might help in the initial stages of reviewing and updating a unit.

<copy/paste a lesson plan into the LLM>. Suggest gaps and silences in this lesson plan.

This seemingly simple prompt can produce some surprising results. The term 'gaps and silences' is often used in Literature studies and the

Humanities when identifying whose voices are 'missing' from a text, and why. Using the terms here will prompt the model to look for perspectives in your lesson plan or unit of work that might be missing.

For example, I tried this prompt with a Year 7 English unit of work on *The Hero's Journey* – a popular approach to studying story structure and characterisation. The model pointed out that the Hero's Journey is a particularly *Western* narrative structure, and that as such some students might find it less accessible. It also suggested a few options to include, such as oral traditions and Japanese Kishōtenketsu.

Using the attached photo as a basis, create three more activities in this style, but focused on <topic>

Using the image-recognition feature of models like ChatGPT and Microsoft Bing, you can effectively scan and refresh hard-copy resources like worksheets and textbooks. This can be great if you have activities which are engaging and work well, but which need some variation. As an alternative to using image recognition, most phones also have optical character recognition built into the camera app: if you point an iPhone camera at text, for example, it gives you the option to copy/paste the text directly from the photo, which can then be used as input into the prompt.

Take this unit of work and change the format to <new unit plan format>. Include <specific features of the updated plan, for example, assessment types>

This prompt may be useful if your school or institution is moving towards a new planning or assessment framework, such as Understanding by Design. For example, you could specify the Understanding by Design framework (from experience, there is enough information in the dataset to 'understand' what this means, but you could add links to websites for more context). You could then request specific details, such as performance assessments.

Reflect and extend

The prompts in this chapter are crafted to facilitate the process of refreshing and updating educational materials, a task that is often time-consuming and complex for educators. Using GenAI, you can efficiently update resources while ensuring alignment with current educational frameworks and standards.

Here are some reflections and potential extensions for these prompts:

- Consider how GenAI can streamline the process of updating resources. How does this technology help maintain the relevance and effectiveness of educational materials?
- Reflect on the balance between using AI for suggestions and retaining your professional judgement and experience in finalising the content.
- Think about the potential for GenAI to identify gaps and biases in existing materials. How might this influence your approach to inclusive and comprehensive education?

And to extend these ideas:

- Combine various prompts to create a more comprehensive process. For instance, start by identifying gaps in a lesson plan, then use another prompt to suggest new activities and, finally, update the entire unit to align with a new teaching framework.
- Explore using GenAI to refresh not just the content, but also the delivery methods of a lesson or unit. For example, incorporate technology or multimedia elements into traditional lesson plans.
- Test the effectiveness of these refreshed resources in a real classroom setting. Gather feedback from students and colleagues to refine and further improve the materials, and compare the 'before and after'.

CHAPTER 19
Improvising

By themselves, current generations of AI can't improvise or be creative – they always rely on some form of input, and they're drawing on a vast but ultimately limited dataset. Humans, on the other hand, have a much greater capacity for creativity and improvisation. Unfortunately, a lot of that goes out of the window when it's 2pm on a Friday and you're confronted with a room of students waiting for the weekend.

Educators are also often confronted with situations where they are teaching out of field, or where a student is looking for advice on a subject area outside of the educator's discipline. In these cases, GenAI can be used to support human creativity and the ability to improvise.

Prompting for improvisation

These prompts draw on a strength of the LLM: its complex and enormous dataset. An LLM has a great capacity for making connections. While you can't use an LLM as a search engine (see page 9 for why not), you can lean on the vast dataset to make surprising and often useful connections across disciplines.

Generate three novel ways to explain nonlinear equations to a grade 10 student at 2pm on a Friday.

This first prompt might seem a little facetious, but LLMs certainly have the capacity to infer that '2pm on a Friday' requires a *simplistic* explanation. You could, of course, just use the word 'simple', but this prompt reinforces some of the points made in earlier role-play prompts: you can use personality traits, emotions and scenarios to shape the output.

Generate seven different scenarios for groups of three students based on <text/topic> and exploring <idea being discussed>. Provide descriptions of each student's role in and the scenario in this format: Scenario name: Scenario description: Student 1 role: Student 2 role: Student 3 role:

GenAI is very useful for generating resources quickly. Sometimes, you need something like this in a hurry to keep a class engaged, or to respond to a sudden idea on the spot. Setting up seven separate scenarios would otherwise take a long time, but this can be done in a matter of seconds.

Generate three possible prompts for a personal response essay exploring the connections between <text> and <student's favourite sport/hobby>

As we'll see in the following chapter, the ability to make connections between topics can often be used effectively to personalise tasks for individual students. This example could be used to generate short, low-stakes writing activities for students to respond to. It could make a useful 'getting to know you' task, but could also be adapted to a more sophisticated piece of writing.

Develop a set of 10 exit questions for a class quiz on <current text/topic>. Ensure that the questions cover a range of difficulty levels and assessment types (for example, multiple choice, short answer, true/false).

Sometimes you just need a quick test of comprehension as students wrap up a topic. Generating 'exit questions' on the fly can be done by including the topic or, even better, some of the course materials in the prompt. Like previous examples of resource creation, you could use a link, an uploaded file or a copy/paste to contextualise this kind of prompt.

Create a list of 10 surprising connections between <topic> and any random ideas. The random ideas should cover a range of areas from science, humanities, politics and the arts.

Again, leveraging the connection-making ability of the LLM, this prompt will likely create connections that you and your students hadn't thought of. It can easily be adapted to tailor the subject disciplines or areas you are building connections with, and could be used as part of tailoring lesson materials to students' interests.

Suggest five ways to explain the concept of <topic> with increasing levels of abstraction.

This prompt might be useful for creating differentiated levels of explanation for a concept or topic in your class. Students may respond to different levels of abstraction. It might also be useful for you to explore new ways of explaining concepts you're familiar with.

Use browsing to search for current events related to <topic>. Provide a list of links and a summary of each article and explain in dot-points how it relates to the topic.

This prompt obviously only works with browsing-enabled applications like Microsoft Bing Chat, but provides an augmented search experience which can be useful for collating materials on current affairs (or anything that crops up during discussions in the classroom). The model will provide links, summaries and explanations which can be quickly scanned for relevance and accuracy.

Reflect and extend

By now, you should be noticing that the best approach to prompting is to be clear about what you want and express it as simply as possible. For improvising prompts, that's especially important as you don't want to be spending lots of time labouring over the exact wording. These prompts are designed to be used off the cuff and even in the middle of a lesson. Here are a few questions to prompt reflection:

- When do you find yourself in situations needing improvisation? What kinds of tools (digital or otherwise) do you usually reach for in these situations?
- How might GenAI be used to support your understanding of a subject area, for example, providing alternative explanations for concepts you are familiar with?

- How might it be used in subject areas you are *unfamiliar* with, such as when teaching a cover class or teaching out of field?

To extend these *improvising* prompts, you might try the following:

- Deliberately build improvisation into your curriculum planning. Combine these prompts with the *planning* and *refreshing* prompts from the previous two chapters and aim for some surprising connections in lesson plans and resources.
- Use these methods in combination with image generation (see Part 5) to create visual stimuli and materials for use in lessons.
- Use the 'connection-making' ability of GenAI to deliberately push you out of your comfort zone. Alternatively, push back against the tendency of LLMs to drift towards generic output by including elements of improvisation in your prompts.

CHAPTER 20
Personalising

Personalising learning using GenAI is one of the most talked about, but also one of the most problematic areas of the technology in education. There are already hundreds of companies claiming to offer 'personalised learning' through chatbots and predictive algorithms, but to date there is little research as to their efficacy. There are also all of the issues of bias and discrimination discussed in Part 2 of this book, which might be amplified when dealing with already-marginalised students.

Instead of relying on GenAI to personalise learning based on its 'understanding' of the student, these prompts rely on the educator and student working together to create resources and approaches which benefit the student. Like other areas of the book, GenAI is used in a supporting role to allow the educator to focus on the more relational aspects of teaching, and as a way to help differentiate and personalise approaches that still rely on the educator's expertise and skills.

Prompts for personalising

These prompts use a variety of methods to adjust learning outcomes, change the complexity or nature of resources, and help students to develop goals using research and evidence-based approaches to differentiation and inclusive education. Remember that the dataset of an LLM, while vast, is incomplete – no dataset reflects the complexity and diversity of our students.

Reproduce this text at a grade 6 level. Keep the original tone, style, ideas and structure: <copy/paste text>

This first prompt offers a very simple way to change the complexity of a text, which is a very common use of GenAI applications like ChatGPT and Microsoft Bing Chat. It's not an exact science – you're relying on the model 'knowing' what that grade/level of writing looks like; however, it does a reasonably good job and can be tweaked with further prompting. Importantly, this prompt attempts to retain the original tone, style, ideas and structure.

STUDENT has an autism diagnosis. STUDENT's individual learning profile currently has three goals: <copy/paste goals>. STUDENT would like to update their goals to reflect ideas from the materials on Universal Design for Learning and inclusive education, and in particular the information from this research: <link to research or attach PDF>. Using the above, create three goals from the student's perspective to help them work with teachers in an inclusive education setting. The goals are written for the student, by the student, in student-friendly language and the first person.

This is a complex prompt that's worth breaking down:

- The student's name is replaced by the word STUDENT. Never use personally identifiable information (PII) in interactions with GenAI.
- The current goals are provided as context and a starting point, providing they don't include any PII (such as information from a medical report).
- The prompt includes reference to research on Universal Design for Learning (UDL) and inclusive education. To do this, the prompt directs the model to a specific piece of research either via a link or an uploaded PDF. Several models, including ChatGPT (paid), Microsoft Bing Chat (free) and Claude (free with limited access) comprise both capabilities.
- The prompt then instructs the model to use the autism diagnosis, existing goals and UDL/inclusive education research to create new goals.
- Finally, the style of the goals is articulated: 'student-friendly language and the first person'.

It's worth noting that much of the content of model training datasets related to disability is likely to be outdated and possibly ableist. For example, I've done a lot of exploration around how LLMs interpret autism and have seen a lot of negative and pathologising information, with little focus on strengths-based approaches or lived experience. This is why a piece of research is used to anchor this prompt.

STUDENT's subjects are English, Maths, Health and PE, Wood, Visual Arts, Music, Indonesian, Science and Humanities. Using STUDENT's goals, the five general modifications and the information from the research, suggest three modification dot-points for each subject teacher.

This is an extension of the previous prompt which uses the information from the goals to create suggested modification for a range of disciplines. These should be negotiated with the student and parent/caregiver.

Design a small-group activity based on a student's passion or interest (for example, music, nature, art). Explain how this activity will engage the student and support their understanding of the content being covered in the lesson.

You don't always need to differentiate because of specific learning needs. Sometimes, it's helpful to align topics with students' particular interests. This prompt could be adapted for groups or individuals.

Create a list of five alternative assessment tasks for a student who struggles with traditional assessments (for example, tests, essays). These tasks should aim to assess the student's knowledge and understanding in a way that better suits their strengths.

Taking a strengths-based approach and acknowledging that examinations and tests don't work for all (or even most) students, this prompt can offer some alternative modes of assessment. Again, you should be on the lookout for 'educational myths' like learning styles (kinaesthetic, auditory, etc), which frequently crop up in the output due to the dataset.

Role play: You are a student with the following learning needs: <copy/paste list>. Review this unit of work and identify any places you might struggle to meet the assessment outcomes: <copy/paste unit plan>

Taking an approach like the *refreshing* chapter, this prompt offers a way to review a unit of work from the perspective of a student. Of course, it doesn't replace talking with your students about their needs, but it can be helpful if you have a class of more than 20 students and need to get some quick feedback.

Clarify this assessment task sheet and break it down into five clear stages. Articulate each stage and what the student needs to do to achieve the expected outcomes: <copy/paste assessment task sheet>

Sometimes, all a student needs is a little clarity over the steps needed to complete an assessment task. Providing students have access to something like ChatGPT or Bing, they can use this prompt themselves.

Reflect and extend

These prompts allow for personalisation of learning resources and the creation of goals working alongside the student, without relying on AI to 'understand' a student. There are very valid concerns over using AI – both predictive and generative – to personalise learning. Predictive algorithms, for example, 'classify' data by labelling and finding patterns in past data and then using those patterns to predict future outcomes. As discussed elsewhere in this book, however, datasets are *always* biased and therefore predictive algorithms may not be able to capture the diversity of our students.

Here are some questions to reflect on when using these types of prompts:

- What would be the most beneficial approach to personalising learning for a given student? Can GenAI assist in changing the complexity of resources or does the student need a more 'human' form of intervention?
- How can you involve the students, parents and caregivers in the process of using AI to personalise learning?

- Does your school/institution have clear and transparent communication around how AI technologies – including generative and predictive – are used to personalise learning?

To extend the ideas in this chapter:

- Find ways to include students in the use of AI to personalise their learning, including showing them how to effectively use the applications.
- Use GenAI to connect students to relevant, contemporary research that is based on lived experience. For example, strengths-based and inclusive research around autism is increasing and moving away from pathologising or deficit-based approaches – students may benefit from accessible versions of this research.
- Always try to measure the efficacy of personalised learning approaches, including regular review of goals that have been developed using approaches like the ones above.

CHAPTER 21
Collaborating

Throughout this book, the focus has been on using GenAI technologies in a supporting role to augment your skills and expertise. You can consider GenAI tools like ChatGPT to be a 'collaborator' in some of your day-to-day tasks with administrative tasks, but also some of the more complex and creative activities.

However, it's also useful to think of ways that GenAI can contribute to collaboration with one another – with our colleagues, students and the broader community. GenAI can be used in ways which facilitate communication (the focus of the following chapter), but also free up time for working together in face-to-face or online groups.

Prompts for collaborating

These prompts are designed to facilitate collaboration – sometimes with the AI, and sometimes with each other. Some involve inviting chatbots into faculty meetings to participate or to take care of administrative tasks. Some of the prompts focus instead on freeing up time to make those meetings more productive. There's a growing and concerning narrative in education that teachers don't need time to meet and collaborate because 'meetings are ineffective' or because teachers should be using off-the-shelf curriculum resources. I disagree. I think that we need to find ways to make the time we spend together more productive and creative.

These are my notes from a professional development on <topic>: <copy/paste notes>. Turn them into an outline for a three-minute oral presentation to report back to my faculty.

Use a prompt like this to share some ideas from professional learning, conferences or things you've learned online. When I was a head of faculty, we often used meeting time to share best practice, run examples of successful activities, and so on.

Role play: You are a member of the school senior leadership team. We are writing a new policy about <policy topic>. Critically appraise this policy, looking for any issues with diversity or representation: <copy/paste policy draft>

As well as faculty-level discussions, GenAI can be used to contribute to other levels of discussion in a school, including the creation of policies and guidelines. Ironically, given the inherent bias in GenAI datasets, it can be prompted to highlight gaps and silences (see the *refreshing* chapter for a similar approach applied to curriculum planning).

We are designing a faculty retreat for half a day where we will work on our scope and sequence and some team building. Suggest an outline for the half day.

Sometimes you just need a little help organising your face-to-face time together. GenAI can be used to support administrative duties, such as planning and scheduling events. You can also prompt it to deliberately avoid any awkward bonding activities...

Translate these materials into <language> and <language> so that a group of students with three different language backgrounds can collaborate on the same task.

Models like OpenAI's GPT and Google's PaLM contain a lot of language data. Google's model can reportedly handle more than 40 languages very competently, and others with decreasing accuracy based on the volume of that language in the dataset. This can be used to support collaboration in the classroom across languages. It's important to note that some languages are underrepresented in models. Sometimes, it's because there is not enough data in the dataset. Other times – such as with Australian First Nations languages – it is because it is not necessarily culturally appropriate to include the language in a dataset.

<Use an AI app like Otter.ai to record and transcribe a meeting, and copy/paste the meeting transcript>. Extract the main actions and important notes from this meeting transcript, and put them into a table alongside the person responsible and a date if one was mentioned.

GenAI does an increasingly good job of transcribing audio, including the use of live speech-to-text software to transcribe meetings. These applications can be used on a mobile or other device, or connected to applications like Zoom. Of course, you always need explicit permission from everyone involved in the meeting. Some platforms like Otter include the capacity to extract key notes, but I find that generally applications like ChatGPT do a slightly better job.

These are the various notes from our discussions in a <topic> meeting: <attach photos of board notes, sticky notes, handwritten notes, etc>. Produce a synthesis of these notes under headings. Use Markdown to format the document under appropriate headings and subheadings.

This prompt takes physical notes and digitises them quickly – again, it's a fairly low-stakes but sometimes time-consuming administrative task to capture this kind of information. It uses the image-recognition capabilities of applications like ChatGPT and Microsoft Bing Chat, which are increasing in accuracy. The prompt also specifies the *formatting* of the output, instructing the model to use Markdown, which is a lightweight programming language that creates headings, bold text and other styles. If you have ChatGPT Plus, you could also ask for this to be exported as a Word document (it will use a module in the programming language python to do this).

<copy/paste transcription of first half of meeting>. Role play: You are a participant in this meeting. Ask five critical questions about the first half of the meeting that we can follow up on in our next discussion.

This combines the transcript of your physical meeting with the 'critical questions' prompt from the *planning* chapter, and might provide some interesting discussion prompts for the second half of the meeting. Meetings don't have to be about ticking administrative boxes – you can also use that time to experiment with these technologies.

Reflect and extend

These prompts have focused on collaborating with the AI and also using GenAI to help you collaborate with each other. Many of these prompts can be adapted for use in the classroom, as long as you have permission for recording if using transcription.

Here are some prompts for reflection on this chapter:

- How can you adapt these prompts to use in a classroom with a group of students, rather than with your colleagues?
- Beyond just 'timesaving', what might be some other advantages of using GenAI for administrative tasks in a group setting?
- What do you *lose* when you offload tasks like transcription and minute-taking to AI?

And to extend:

- In the (near) future, it's likely that GenAI applications will be competent enough with speech-to-text and text-to-speech that they can participate 'live' in meetings in ways like this. Consider the implications of privacy and data security, but also potential creative applications of this technology.
- Combine the approaches in this chapter with techniques from Part 5 of this book, where we'll look at image generation. How can images be used in collaborative contexts?
- Code interpreter was briefly mentioned in one prompt for creating a Word document. You can create many file formats in the code interpreter model (ChatGPT Plus), including PowerPoints, spreadsheets and files that interact with software like calendar apps. Invest some time learning how to collaborate with the more powerful aspects of applications like ChatGPT.

CHAPTER 22
Communicating

The final strategy, *communicating*, leans into the fact that LLMs are basically just machines for generating a lot of text. As educators, we're constantly communicating with each other, our students, parents and caregivers, and the community. GenAI isn't going to replace human communication anytime soon, but it might take some of the stress out of certain communications.

GenAI is also very useful for changing the tone, style and form of language, such as converting documents into other formats, reusing communications materials or creating new means of communicating with a broader audience.

Prompts for communicating

These prompts all rely on some initial input and then human revision. We don't want to use applications like ChatGPT to generate all of our communications without checking their quality, accuracy and relevance. They can also take varied forms of input, including student (or parent/caregiver, or staff) survey data, and communicate the results effectively in a range of forms.

Rewrite this email to make it neutral and not accusatory: <copy/paste email draft>

A simple prompt that you *hopefully* won't have to use too often. GenAI is very good at 'neutralising' the tone of writing. In fact, trained chatbot applications like ChatGPT are a little *too good* at writing in a bland, neutral voice.

Draft an email to parents of <class> to congratulate the students on their efforts on the recent field trip. Here is a newsletter article about the field trip for context: <copy/paste newsletter article>

It's always best to provide context for this kind of prompt, otherwise you will get a very generic response. I've worked in schools where they have surveyed parents and caregivers and asked which kinds of communications might use GenAI, and where they would prefer the technology not to be used. Generally, parents and caregivers don't mind if GenAI is used for short updates and reflections, but they don't really want it to be used as part of high-stakes feedback and reporting.

Use the following feedback from students to create a script for an assembly item reflecting on the recent visit from <incursion>: <copy/paste survey form responses>

This prompt uses data in one form – a student survey – to produce materials of another. You can copy/paste an entire column from a spreadsheet of answers from Google Forms or a similar platform if it has no identifying information. In some models, you can just upload the spreadsheet or CSV file directly and the model can extract the data from the file.

Draft a report to the school community from the Director of Learning and Teaching, which focuses on the following achievements this year: <list of achievements>

Again, this prompt uses existing information to contextualise a new piece of writing. This could also be an assembly item, a presentation to the board or any other form of communication.

Compile a list of talking points to share with new teachers during an orientation session. The talking points should highlight the school's values, mission and learning philosophy: <copy/paste school mission information>

School and university onboarding processes often leave a lot to be desired. I've been 'onboarded' into many organisations and left confused and disoriented. GenAI could be used to make that whole process clearer. Using processes like retrieval augmented generation, chatbots can increasingly be connected to an organisation's database of internal documents, which would make this kind of communication even easier.

Create a script for a podcast that celebrates the achievements of the school community. The podcast should showcase the efforts of students, staff and families, based on the following notes: <copy/paste notes>

This prompt offers a way to turn a pile of notes from various members of the community into something much more engaging and unique. It might be used by a school or organisation's marketing or development office, or as part of an assembly or other event.

Read and respond to this email succinctly, but politely: <copy/paste email with no identifying information>

Finally, a simple prompt to take some of the mental load out of responding to countless emails.

Reflect and extend

This final strategy demonstrates GenAI's ability to play around with form, tone and writing style. Because of the huge dataset, there is a lot of capacity in GenAI models to 'play' with language. However, it also tends to drift towards a very neutral and frankly dull communication style. Sometimes, 'neutral' is exactly what you need.

Here are some final reflection questions:

- What kinds of communication *shouldn't* you use GenAI for?
- Will your organisation develop policies or guidelines around how GenAI is and isn't to be used in the public sphere?
- How are your students permitted to use GenAI in communications with staff and with each other? Where do you teach them how?

And to extend this strategy:

- Think of ways you can use combinations of technology, as explored in earlier chapters, with AI-assisted transcription tools and speech-to-text.

- The methods in this chapter can be very useful for taking one original text – for example, a written article – and converting it into multiple forms of communication. Think about how you might save time and redundancy by using one text in multiple ways.
- Talk to your organisation's marketing team – they're the experts in communication and might offer some surprising ways that you could use the ideas in this chapter.

PART 5
Practical strategies for image generation

In this part of the book, I'm going to explore image generation. Obviously, this printed text (or eBook) isn't the ideal place for including lots of images, so I'd recommend that you check out all the original posts for the full-size, full-colour images. Image generation has come a *long* way in the past 12 months, and you really do need to experience it for yourself.

There are also many ethical issues with AI image generation, some of which were discussed in Part 2. These include the infringement of intellectual property and copyright, the use of image generation to create deepfakes, and the impact on the artistic and creative industries. You'll need to decide for yourself where you stand on these complex ethical issues.

I use several different platforms for image generation. In educational contexts, I'd recommend sticking to Microsoft Bing Image Creator and Adobe Firefly, since they have the most robust guardrails and security features. Adobe's model is trained exclusively on Adobe Stock images, public domain content and images shared under open licences. Nothing under copyright has gone into the training, unlike other models. Adobe does not use its customers' content (photos and artwork stored on the Creative Cloud servers, for example) unless they are added to Adobe Stock.

Images generated with Firefly are tagged with metadata that identifies them as AI content, and they have worked on new licensing for AI-generated images. This is an important step for transparency and avoiding the spread of deepfake or harmful images with GenAI.

The technology has also been built into Photoshop, as well as a few extra features, such as Generative Fill and Generative Expand. Many schools have Adobe Creative Cloud licences and/or Photoshop available for students, so Firefly is available through a simple email login with a school email address. In terms of privacy and student data, this means that students do not need to use a personal email account, and that logins can be centrally administered within the school.

Writing prompts for image generation

Writing prompts for image-generation models used to be fairly complex, and platforms like Midjourney still involve a certain level of understanding of codes and conventions. For example, in Midjourney you need to use codes like --ar 16:9 for a widescreen aspect ratio or --no to exclude ideas from the final image.

Increasingly, however, image models use the same natural language features of LLMs. With Bing Chat, for example, you can 'chat' with the model to get it to generate the image you're looking for. In ChatGPT Plus (the paid product), you can use a very vague prompt and the model will write its own image-generation prompt in response.

All the general prompting advice from the previous part of this book applies to image generation, but you should also be aware of the following dos and don'ts:

- Do use descriptive, rich language in your prompt.
- Do refer to movements and aesthetic styles as well as form and media.
- Do use surprising and unusual language just to play around with the output.
- Don't prompt for images of real people, living or dead. Prompts for living people will often be rejected and prompts for deceased individuals might be unethical.
- Don't prompt for the styles of artists – instead, try to use language which is precise and conveys what you're really looking for.
- Don't try to generate unsafe or explicit content – all the models discussed in this book will reject such requests anyway.

To make your image generation more interesting, use vocabulary that draws on various art styles, media, movements and expressive language. This would be a good time to tap your Visual Arts colleagues on the shoulder and ask for advice, or maybe the Media or Film Studies department. Here are some vocabulary terms to get you started.

Mix and match the terms in your prompts and see what you can come up with. In a chatbot-based image generator like ChatGPT or Bing, it will do some of the work for you even with very vague prompts. In a model like Adobe Firefly, you will need to use more specific language. Firefly also has little toggles that you can flick on and off that handle different styles, media, and so on.

Artistic movements	Photography styles	Artistic and film media	Visual/aesthetic elements
Renaissance	Portrait	Painting	Bold lines
Baroque	Landscape	Drawing	Film grain
Rococo	Street	Printmaking	Vivid colour
Neoclassicism	Documentary	Sculpture	Bokeh
Romanticism	Fashion	Photography	HDR
Realism	Architectural	Installation art	Chiaroscuro
Impressionism	Sports	Textile arts	Monochrome
Post-Impressionism	Wildlife	Ceramics	Texture
Fauvism	Astrophotography	Glass art	Negative space
Expressionism	Macro	Digital art	Perspective
Cubism	Food	Narrative film	Symmetry
Futurism	Still life	Documentary film	Vignetting
Dada	Abstract	Animated film	Double exposure
Surrealism	Fine art	Experimental film	Selective focus
Abstract Expressionism	Black and white	Silent film	Sepia tone

Like the previous strategies for GenAI language-based models, this part of the book breaks image generation into six strategies that educators can incorporate into their day-to-day work:

1. Critiquing
2. Sketching
3. Designing
4. Visualising
5. Storyboarding
6. Creating

Obviously, it's difficult to convey the quality of AI-generated images in a black and white book (unless you're reading the full-colour eBook), so I'd recommend you search for the original blog post. Google *Leon Furze Practical Strategies for Image Generation* and you'll find it.

Figure 5: 'Abstract Impressionist architectural photograph capturing a Gothic cathedral. The image should emphasise bokeh effects' – prompt generated by ChatGPT using words from the vocabulary table

CHAPTER 23
Critiquing

Like I've said previously, datasets don't reflect reality. They amplify biases in reality.

There are under- and over-representations of gender, race, age, disability, sexuality and culture throughout image datasets. That doesn't necessarily mean we shouldn't use them, but it does mean we should be aware of what we're using. The issue of bias in datasets is also very teachable. Before you go into any of the other strategies, I'd suggest that you try a few experiments for yourself to identify some of the visible and hidden biases in image-generation tools. The easiest way to do this is to think of stereotyped roles, occupations or stereotypical images of race, gender, sexuality and disability, and prompt image-generation platforms to create a photo.

Some examples I've used in the past include CEO, scientist, autistic person, disabled person, teacher, woman, man and parent. You'll find that the more recent models, like Firefly and Bing, have started to address the issues that crop up in public models, such as open-source models like Stable Diffusion, and earlier models like DALL·E 2. Unfortunately, those fixes are often a band-aid over the top of the real problem, which is the representation in the dataset.

The best thing you can do is get in there, experiment and figure out for yourself who is and who is not represented in the outputs from the image generation. Once you've got that, you know what to do about it. It is possible to deliberately design prompts that represent more diverse images. Sometimes, image generation will struggle to generate images that are outside of the bounds of the dataset, but most of the time you can successfully prompt for more diverse images.

Think about your school community: you, your colleagues, your students, parents and caregivers, and the whole community your school is situated in. Chances are that the diverse population of your school community isn't represented in the limited datasets of image models. So, what can you do about it? When generating images, be mindful to deliberately include language to generate diverse groups that are more representative of your context.

Prompts for critiquing

Photo of a CEO

The classic 'CEO test' for image generation. Try it in a few different models to see what kinds of guardrails (if any) have been applied.

Image of a group of people

Results may vary. Look under the hood at DALL·E 3 prompts, used in applications like ChatGPT and Microsoft Bing Chat. You'll often see that the model adds descriptive terms like 'a diverse group of people of mixed ages, ethnicities and gender' to 'fix' the diversity problems from the dataset.

Image of a <person representing a minority>

This prompt will allow you to explore how minority groups are represented – or not – in various models. It can result in some very disappointing and even concerning outputs depending on the representation you're seeking. For example, 'image of an autistic person' in Midjourney always results in young males depicted in distress, often surrounded by darkness and 'puzzle piece' iconography, which is a problematic symbol used by an American organisation that obviously features heavily in the dataset.

Figure 6: 'Photo of a CEO' generated in Midjourney

CHAPTER 24
Sketching

Off the ethical high horse and onto an image-generation use that's genuinely fun and has many practical applications. There is a new feature of Bing Chat that uses OpenAI's GPT-4 vision (GPT-4v) model for image recognition. It doesn't always get things right, but like all of these technologies, it will continue to improve. One thing it excels at is taking sketches and turning them into fully realised images.

If you're planning resources and have an idea in your head that you might not find on Google image search, try a quick napkin sketch. Take a photo with your phone, throw it into Bing Chat, ask it what it sees, correct it if necessary and then generate the image. In the prompt, ensure you specify to use the sketch as a reference. Or, if you're teaching a Design and Technology or Arts subject and you're looking to illustrate the process from design to a more finished product, you could use a quick sketch in this manner.

Think of occasions where this strategy might be beneficial in your day-to-day job, particularly around producing resources, sketching out ideas for colleagues or making images that would be hard to find in a Google image search. Try a few sketches through Bing Chat.

Prompts for sketching

These prompts rely on a model that has image-recognition features, such as ChatGPT or Microsoft Bing Chat.

Turn this image into a full-colour piece of digital art: <upload sketch>

This will create an interpretation of the original sketch and will produce something that is fairly close in terms of style, theme and composition.

Turn this sketch into a realistic photograph. The image should be as photo realistic as possible, ultra-high quality, lots of detail: <upload sketch>

Like the previous prompt, this will convert the sketch to an image. However, the language in this prompt is much more specific and should result in a more realistic output. At the time of writing, DALL·E (used in both ChatGPT and Microsoft Bing Chat) still tends towards a quite 'computer-generated' look.

Turn this idea into a real product: <copy/paste sketch>

Useful for design ideas, this prompt will take a sketch and turn it into a finished render of a product. Adding more detail to the prompt will make it even closer to the finished idea.

Figure 7: Sketch of a cat turned into digital art by Bing Chat

CHAPTER 25
Designing

As well as using image generation for sketch-to-prototype as part of the design process, there are many elements of design in technologies, graphic design, media, visual arts, visual communication and similar subjects. Both teachers and students are expected to use digital technologies to produce layouts, artwork, and so on.

For example, a task might require students to design and prototype an app for a mobile phone or a smartphone. Or perhaps website design is part of a STEM or computer science course, including the creation of banners and header images for websites. Like the sketch example earlier, product design and technology and visual arts courses might also use GenAI as an element of the design process.

Do you teach a subject or topic where you require students to design something from scratch, including the visuals? It might be best for you, as the educator, to model the process. Identify a few places where, instead of using traditional graphic design software, you might employ GenAI in the process.

Prompts for designing

These prompts revolve around using fast, creative methods to quickly design and iterate on ideas.

Smartphone app design, app screen, environmental sustainability app, calm and vibrant.

Swap out 'environmental sustainability' and you have a very quick prototype of a mobile phone application that could form part of any project. At the moment, this could simply be an idea or a 'what if', but pretty soon it will be possible to use GenAI to fully realise the entire application (see Part 6 of this book for more on code, 3D and the future of AI).

Create concept art sketches for <a new product or idea>.

Concept art sketches look fantastic, and the artists that create them often have highly expressive styles that can convey movement, energy and emotion. I, on the other hand, would find it difficult to convey some of my design ideas in such an eloquent way. But I can express myself in writing, and I could use a prompt like this to create some impressive concept art sketches.

Design a website including the layout, colour scheme and placement of particular items. The website is for a school science fair, and is intended to promote the fair to the community.

In Part 6, I've got a screenshot of a 'sketch to website' concept, much like the prompts used in the previous chapter. But you can also let the GenAI do a little more of the work and generate complete design ideas. This could be great for rapid prototyping, or just when you - or your students - are stuck for ideas.

Figure 8: Designing a phone app in Adobe Firefly

CHAPTER 26
Visualising

Being able to imagine a concept, visualise it and express it as an illustration, visual collage, portfolio, lookbook or mood board is an element of many disciplines. Visualising might involve simply imagining what a concept looks like, or it could involve visualising different components of a larger product. For example, you might use GenAI to create a mood board or colour board as an alternative to using a platform like Pinterest (which is often blocked on school networks because it constitutes social media).

You might want to use GenAI for visualising as part of your planning process: if you're developing a new curriculum, creating resources, preparing something for the school community like a newsletter, or contributing to school social media or a website, and you want to visualise what some of this might look like ahead of time.

Prompts for visualising

These prompts take abstract ideas and make them more concrete, or help your students to get over the threat of the blank page by providing more ways to get the images in their minds down on paper.

Create a mood board for a new art curriculum.

Use descriptive language to clearly describe the themes, emotions and visual elements you are imagining. This prompt helps in visualising and presenting a coherent concept for a new curriculum, and can incorporate various art styles, historical periods or cultural influences.

Generate a colour palette and imagery for <an upcoming school event>

Specify the event's theme, atmosphere and target audience. You can use a prompt like this for creating themes that line up with the event's purpose and audience.

Illustrate a <complex abstract concept>

Describe a scientific principle, experiment or abstract concept in as much detail as possible or use GenAI to create a vivid description, and use that as the basis for the image. This prompt helps in visualising theoretical concepts or experimental setups, making them more accessible and understandable for students. As well as science experiments or concepts, you could, for example, use this in a subject like Literature to visualise a complex term.

Figure 9: ChatGPT's (DALL·E 3) slightly concerning attempt to visualise emotions

CHAPTER 27
Storyboarding

Storyboarding might seem like a technique limited to the English or Media classroom, but it's a very useful tool in many areas. You can use storyboarding to outline presentations, assemblies, create a narrative that supports a school event or as an activity in the classroom. I've collaborated with Science teachers who use storyboarding as a means to demonstrate lab processes, Design and Technology teachers to step through practical lessons, and Health and PE teachers to visually guide students through training plans.

With image generation, you don't need to spend a long time searching through Google for images, nor do you need significant artistic talent. Combining this with the sketch strategy from earlier can help you quickly generate images for a visual storyboard for any of those applications.

Think beyond the confines of the English classroom when considering storyboarding. If you're in a school leadership role and you ever need to deliver a presentation – be it to your colleagues, the rest of the leadership team, parents, caregivers or the community – then creating a storyboard can be an impactful way to convey your points and even to organise your own thoughts.

Prompts for storyboarding

Create a panel for a storyboard as black and white line art to explain the first stage of preparing a meal: gathering the ingredients.

Use simple art styles like black and white line art to add a little clarity to procedural writing, such as the steps of cooking a meal or setting up an experiment.

In a photorealistic style, create six panels of a storyboard for a short promotional video demonstrating the best features of the school English faculty. The photos should be of areas of the school such as the library (a fun, contemporary library, not an old-fashioned or traditional library).

Be as descriptive as you like when creating images. You might not get what you want on the first (or second, or third) try, but you'll often end up with a few surprises along the way. ChatGPT and Bing Chat will create a sequence of images one after the other if you instruct them to do so, whereas in other models you will need to create the images separately.

Create step-by-step images for a physical education training plan based on the following information: <copy/paste training plan>.

As with other prompts, you can provide contextual information or, in the case of an internet connected application, send the model off to look at websites for inspiration before generating a sequence of images.

Figure 10: Bold black line art storyboard of an English faculty generated in Bing Chat

CHAPTER 28
Creating

I left this strategy to the end because it's the most obvious: image generation can be used to create images! The number of different ways educators might create images is too vast to try to capture in this chapter. Some of the most obvious reasons educators might create images include making resources for PowerPoints, handouts and activities, creating images for social media, school websites, newsletters and other communications, and so on.

In some subjects, it might also be useful to create images as stimulus materials or prompts, such as in creative writing, or as reference images in the arts. The key part of this strategy is to just let your imagination run free. Anytime you find yourself navigating to an image search, think about what it is you're picturing and why you want to find that image. Then try to create a short prompt which captures that to use in Firefly or Bing.

Sometimes you'll get outputs that are pretty weird. Sometimes you'll get something that's incredibly similar to what you were imagining. And often, you'll find that you're able to create images that you could never find through a traditional search.

Instead of giving specific prompts here, I want you to think of some of your own!

Refer to the table of vocabulary on page 137 and create some interesting combinations of aesthetic style, media, descriptive language, and so on. Like many of the technologies covered in this book, the best way to learn is to get in there and play around.

Figure 11: Using Adobe to play around with creative forms and styles

PART 6
The future of GenAI

Obviously, I don't have a crystal ball. And, given how this technology has advanced in the past 12 months, it might seem ridiculous to try to predict what the next three or five years have in store for these technologies. But although GPT-3 accelerated the adoption of LLMs, it's not a particularly new technology, and some elements are following particular curves.

In this part of the book, I'll be exploring some of the most likely near-future trends with these technologies and discussing the implications for education. We'll also look at some of the GenAI models not really discussed elsewhere in this book, including audio, video and code generation. The first two are not as advanced as text and image generation in terms of quality and accessibility, but they're not far behind.

Code generation has been used in computer science and software industries for much longer than GPT-3 has been around. But it's not yet a huge component of education because outside of Digital Technologies and occasionally Mathematics or Science, not many teachers are prepared to work with code. However, the combination of text, image, audio, video, code and 3D asset generation are rapidly converging and are likely to have huge implications for augmented and virtual reality technologies, including technologies which are gaining traction in education.

I'll also explore the idea of autonomous agents, which certain members of the technology and AI community believe will be the next logical step in AI. I'm going to steer clear of the existential threat narrative that has dominated media discourse and is being promoted by some prominent figures in AI. A recent AI summit in the UK, for example, focused on the threat to humanity, including acts of terrorism and warfare, artificial general intelligence (AGI) or artificial superintelligence (ASI) taking over the world.

I side with many AI scholars and ethicists who believe that these existential threat narratives are mainly a distraction from the real here and now risks, including the ethical concerns. In education, I think we'd be far better off focusing on the present-day problems of the technology and not wasting our time on risks that might never come to fruition. That doesn't mean

I don't think there are threats inherent in the future of this technology; along with those ethical concerns of bias and environmental impact, the near future will almost certainly have issues as AI is used to automate many jobs.

But this book is focused on the practical applications of GenAI in education, so I'm not going to get too bogged down in those issues. My hope is that by the time you've finished reading this final part of the book, you'll not only be prepared to use the technologies as they exist right now, but also prepared to start thinking about the implications of GenAI for your profession, your subject discipline, and your own passions and interests in the short-term future. I also hope you'll be more confident in having conversations with students about the implications of these technologies for future academic and career pathways.

CHAPTER 29
Do we all need to be prompt engineers now?

GenAI is already having an impact across many industries, and although we're definitely in a hype cycle, it's safe to say that many jobs will permanently change or be automated by the technologies. It's too soon to say exactly how this will pan out, but there are some obvious considerations. I work with a lot of secondary schools and speak to students, teachers, parents and caregivers, and there are some real fears about what AI will do to future careers. There's also a lot of misinformation and hyperbole muddying the waters, so in this chapter I hope to clear that up and provide advice on how to discuss these issues with young people.

Let's start with some of the more famous reports that have emerged in 2023 about GenAI and jobs. One of the most widely circulated comes from Goldman Sachs (Briggs & Kodnani, 2023), which indicated 300 million jobs – 18% of the global workforce – could be automated. The report also stated that 'white collar' jobs in finance, business, law, and so on would be the most heavily affected, as opposed to previous technological revolutions which automated manual labour. The numbers might sound daunting, but it's important to recognise that many jobs won't simply disappear; instead, they'll have aspects which can be automated and parts which still need human oversight or thought.

Similar reports from Deloitte Australia and McKinsey (Deloitte Australia, 2023; McKinsey & Company, 2023) indicate upwards of US$600bn of disruption to the economy, and 30% of all jobs potentially automated away. Again, these are big, scary numbers and make it seem as though there will be hardly enough careers left to go around by the time our students are leaving education. I like to take a balanced view of these things. GenAI, including applications like ChatGPT and Adobe's Firefly, will clearly have an impact and will make some jobs redundant. They will also open up other jobs and augment existing jobs in ways which we can't quite foresee.

Glass half empty: the AI workforce dystopia

There are many 'dystopian' possibilities for future career pathways with AI, some of them influenced by jobs which already exist. For example:

- The worsening of the 'gig economy': gig work like Uber driving or Amazon's Mechanical Turk crowdsourcing platform might get more and more prevalent, leading to lots of low-paid, insecure work.
- Data labelling and classification: already, the labelling of AI data is a huge industry which particularly impacts poorer communities. These AI models are hungry for data, and may need more and more human labour.

AI replaces the 'good stuff'; in the games design industry, we've already seen cases where illustrators have been fired, replaced with AI image generation, and then rehired on a lower wage to edit and correct the AI's mistakes.

Glass half full: protecting human creativity and ingenuity

It's not all doom and gloom, however. Here are a few ways AI could open up interesting new careers and pathways:

- AI is being used to take the hard work out of navigating government systems, making it easier for unemployed people, single mothers, disabled people and gig workers to find secure employment.
- Creative industry jobs in AI will continue to evolve, including the use of AI in existing industry standard platforms like Adobe Photoshop.
- New roles and opportunities are opening up in organisations across the world looking for support in both the technical and the ethical aspects of AI and related technologies.

So, what can we do right now?

We might be working with students who won't leave formal education until 2030, so it seems a long way off and can be hard to project forward. That's especially true when you consider how fast some of these technologies are developing. Rather than worrying about which jobs and industries will be 'automated away' by AI, we need to focus our conversations on the capabilities of the technology, the parts of jobs which can be outsourced to AI and which skills we want to remain as uniquely human.

Rather than thinking about entire jobs or industries that might be supplanted by AI, it's better to think of which *tasks* within a job can be handed over. This sounds like a conversation that could easily be transferred into the careers classroom. Talk to students about which tasks can be easily automated, such as low-level administrative work, simple content generation, basic customer service roles. Then discuss the more complex skills – such as those covered by the Australian Curriculum general capabilities – which are much harder to automate.

Future skills

There's already plenty of talk in schools about 'future skills', '21st-century skills', and so on. Unfortunately, it is often just talk. Many schools suffer under a traditional discipline-based curriculum which divides up knowledge into neat subject areas and focuses on the assessment of the content rather than the skills. That approach hasn't worked well for a long time, and the advances in AI may be the final nail in the coffin. However, AI won't revolutionise the education system. Learning how to write lesson plans with chatbots or replacing PowerPoint with Gamma isn't going to change the system.

People can do that, though.

I wrote in Part 3 about the implications of GenAI for assessment, including the need to rethink how we assess knowledge. GenAI can't be effectively banned or detected, and many jobs already require an understanding of the tools and technologies. The education system we have is remarkably resilient and resistant to change, partly because it's incredibly effective at doing what it does. Unfortunately, 'what it does' – ranking students based on narrow measures of intelligence to make it easy to categorise students for post-schoolwork and education – is not aligned with what students do once they leave.

You can throw all the EdTech and AI at this system you like, and it will only reinforce the system. 'Personalised learning', for example, is a snappy catchphrase that's being used a lot in the context of AI chatbots. Applied to the current system, these chatbots will reinforce pathways through standardised testing and high-stakes exams, and the students with access to the best chatbots (read: access to more money) will succeed. People need to make decisions that will change the system before trying to apply technology to it.

CHAPTER 30
The future of multimodal GenAI

We've already explored text generation and image generation in detail, and in Part 4, I touched on code generation, and particularly GPT's ability to write and execute code. In this chapter, I'm going to focus more on some of the burgeoning multimodal technologies, how they work and the implications for education. Increasingly, GenAI like GPT can generate multimodal content that goes beyond text and images, including audio, video and 3D assets, such as objects that can be used in games and virtual reality.

What is multimodality?

Let me indulge in a bit of theory for a moment around what multimodality actually means. I base my definition primarily on the work of literacy scholar Gunther Kress, and particularly his texts *Literacy in the New Media Age* (2003) and *Multimodality* (2010). Kress's definitions of multimodality also informed earlier versions of the Australian curriculum. And although approaches to teaching multimodal texts have never been wholly explicated in the curriculum, I think we need a clear definition and some language with which to discuss GenAI.

Kress's definition of multimodality describes an approach that recognises the many different modes of communication beyond just language. According to Kress, multimodality includes a variety of *semiotic* modes like images, gestures, music, speech and writing, each of which contributes to the meaning-making process. In Kress's view, communication and representation are not solely about language. Instead, they involve a complex interplay of different modes that work together to convey meaning. This perspective is particularly significant in the contemporary world where digital media and technology have led to an increased use of visual and other non-linguistic modes of communication.

Kress also used the terms 'transformation' and 'transduction' to discuss how meaning is shifted within the same mode and across modes. Transformation, for example, refers to information within a single mode being adapted from one text to another; for example, a written short story being transformed into a written play. The mode of delivery, writing versus performance, might change, but the actual mode of the text stays the same. Transduction, on the other hand, involves moving information from one form, one mode, into another. And it's transduction that I'm particularly interested in when it comes to GenAI.

As you saw in Part 5, it's possible to create images from text. The better your prompt or description is, the more accurate the model's interpretation. This is a great example of *transduction* from the written mode to the visual. Artists do this all the time, such as John Everett Millais' 1851 painting *Ophelia*, based on Shakespeare's *Hamlet*. What makes GenAI different, of course, is that the human writes the prompt, but the actual creation of the visual is algorithmically determined by a combination of the user's input images and the construction and training of the model.

Extending Kress's definition of multimodality into GenAI means accounting for some of these methods of transduction and transformation. Obviously, I'm interested in this from an academic point of view. But I feel that there are some very important reasons that we should all be paying attention to the multimodality of GenAI. Multimodal texts are more compelling, more engaging and typically more persuasive than text in a single mode. Various studies have demonstrated, for example, that video, visual and auditory modes combine in more persuasive written text. Similarly, pictures can be more persuasive than audio.

When GPT was first released in November 2022, there were concerns about using the technology to generate fake news on an unprecedented scale. We've certainly seen that this is possible, with entire news websites featuring AI-generated content done with malicious intent and some which simply mislead. Combine the text-creation efforts of GPT with multimodal GenAI, such as the audio and video technologies you'll see in this part of the book, and all of a sudden, the potential for fake news, misinformation and deepfakes becomes much more problematic.

Aside from these obvious issues, however, there are, of course, positive potentials of the technology. Digital technologies, such as the internet, social media, blogs and vlogs, have had many affordances in making communications more accessible, affordable and easier for a greater population. Although we tend to focus on the negative aspects of social media, it has been used in part to overthrow autocratic regimes, for communications during natural and man-made disasters, and for connecting loved ones across the world. Similarly, GenAI, and especially multimodal GenAI, has huge potential for increasing the accessibility and opportunities for people to create text.

Technology is always a balance between potential harms and potential benefits. To be too deterministic and say AI will revolutionise education or destroy education is an oversimplification. Technology by itself doesn't *do* anything. But it isn't neutral, either – technology companies and developers make choices which influence how we use these tools. If a particular multimodal GenAI platform rises to dominance as the creators' tool of choice, just as Instagram and TikTok have as tools for Gen Z to tell their stories, the company that owns that technology has a certain amount of influence over what its users can say. The purpose of education is to ensure everyone has access to the understanding and skills to be able to make their own choices of how they use them.

CHAPTER 31
Audio generation

Audio GenAI tools are built on a similar premise to other forms: take a pile of data, run it through an algorithm to 'learn' the rules of the form and then generate novel content. In the case of audio, this might involve music, speech and sound effects.

Like other forms of GenAI, audio generation is also not without ethical concerns. Privacy and security worries are the most prominent, with audio voices having the potential to breach security measures like telephone banking. Deepfake voices of celebrities are already causing trouble, and fake voices could be used in phone scams by fooling people that their friends and family are calling. Finally, music generation is just as contentious as art generation when it comes to the potential for displacing artists and being used to replace human creators.

In this chapter, I'll explore some of the currently available tools, discuss how they work and what they might be used for, and explore some of the potential issues.

Music generation

Google MusicLM

Although voice synthesis is the most talked about form of GenAI, music models also have great potential to impact the commercial and creative worlds. Google's MusicLM was released in 2023, with a model that can turn text prompts into music samples at 24kHz, and can also generate music based on "whistled and hummed melodies" (according to the research paper – we can't yet do that in the public demo).

To access the MusicLM demo, you have to be registered for Google's AI Test Kitchen, its controlled environment for testing new GenAI products.

Earlier in the year, the AI Test Kitchen saw the first release of what would later become the Bard conversational chatbot. Google's MusicLM examples page demonstrates a range of features and uses that aren't yet available through the demo, such as using a chain of prompts to create a consistent soundtrack that moves from one style to another. However, given the progress in previous demos, it's almost certain that MusicLM will be turned into a fully featured product at some stage and included in the multimodal Gemini model released in December 2023.

Stable Audio

Stable Audio is a new product from Stability AI, the open-source developer behind the powerful Stable Diffusion image model. Stability AI has come under fire for its use of intellectual property in building its image-generation model, and because the model is open source and has no guardrails, it can be used to generate explicit and harmful content. It's interesting, therefore, to look at the approach that's been taken with the audio model. Stability AI has made it very clear where the dataset comes from for Stable Audio: "Our first audio AI model is exclusively trained on music provided by AudioSparx, a leading music library and stock audio website."

Because it only uses stock music, it also can't be used to create music 'in the style of...', one of the most problematic features of its image generation. It seems that this time around, it is trying to avoid a few lawsuits (or if I'm being less cynical, trying to build a more ethical product). Diverging from the fully open-source release of Stable Diffusion, there is also a paid 'pro' version of Stable Audio, which allows for more generations and tracks up to 90 seconds that can be licenced for commercial use. There are a few more controls, including the ability to change the track duration (from 1–45 seconds) and the model, although at the moment only one model exists. Stable Audio can also be used to generate sound effects.

Speech recognition, generation and language translation

Speech recognition and generation use different processes but represent two sides of the same coin. The kind of speech recognition that has powered assistants like Siri and Alexa for years has now advanced to a much more 'human-level' recognition, including complex accents and dialects, slurred or distorted speech, and speech with lots of background noise.

OpenAI's Whisper, for example, is "trained on 680,000 hours of multilingual and multitask supervised data collected from the web" and presents a highly accurate model of speech recognition. It's built into the ChatGPT app if you want to try it out – you'll see right away that it's much more accurate than the iPhone's Siri (pre-iOS 17 at least).

Google has a similarly powerful model with AudioPaLM, Amazon's Alexa has been updated with AI and Apple's Siri will follow soon enough. ElevenLabs has pulled ahead with voice generation, offering a free "instant" version of voice cloning and a premium version which takes "up to four weeks" to generate using longer samples. It also provides totally synthetic voices for commercial use. On my website, I've created a synthetic deepfake of my own voice and used it to produce short, fake, podcast episodes and videos.

GenAI audiobooks

In 2023, there was a media storm when it was revealed that Spotify had provided human audiobook narrators' voices to Apple for use in training its AI model. The big fear, of course, is that ultimately, the real voice actors will be put out of work by the AI. In fact, that's already happening in projects that use AI to narrate out of copyright classics to make free audiobooks (Whitney, 2023).

You could also argue this technology will make texts more accessible, either by making audiobooks free or by adding voiceover to any text online. There's also a chance that real, verified human narration will start to fetch premium prices over low- or no-cost AI, and that professional voice artists might benefit as a result. Again, there are plenty of potential positives and negatives to GenAI audio.

GenAI audio translation

A combination of voice recognition, voice synthesis and text generation can be used to create very accurate language translation models. These models use voice recognition and speech-to-text to convert spoken words into another language, and then use voice synthesis (deepfakes) to produce the new language translation as audio. Increasingly, they can even do a convincing job of lip-syncing over videos. This means you can record a video in one language, and have it almost instantly converted into another language which still looks and sounds like you are saying the words. Various applications, such as HeyGen and Synthesia, were experimenting with these technologies at the time of writing.

Like everything else GenAI related, the audio genie isn't getting stuffed back into the bottle anytime soon. We can expect to see a glut of apps and services built on speech recognition and generation models. Some will be great; others will be next to useless. Many will come with privacy and security concerns, and will be used in ways which are unethical or even criminal. The technology will also be used creatively to produce videos and audio, and in ways which improve accessibility and lower the cost of accessing information in an audio format. It's down to us to decide what role we want these tools to play in our lives.

CHAPTER 32
Video generation

Video generation is still early days at the time of writing, but like all other areas of GenAI, it is rapidly improving and garnering a lot of attention (and money). Obviously, I can't convey all of this in a book, so I would recommend you check out the original blog post I wrote about my experiments with video generation here: leonfurze.com/2023/11/06/hands-on-with-video-generation.

I'm using two platforms in that blog post: Runway and Pika. Runway is leading in terms of quality and the range of tools on offer. In fact, it's building towards an entire editing suite, and beyond video generation it offers editing tools similar to the AI-powered Generative Fill and Expand Adobe products, and more standard tools like colour correction, depth of field adjustments and subtitling. Pika is, like Midjourney, currently found inside Discord. It includes the ability to generate images from text, or to 'animate' still images which you provide.

Both platforms are built on the same premise: a Stable Diffusion-based image-generation model, with motion added. Runway's Gen-1 relied on existing videos, editing the frames directly. Gen-2, which has recently been upgraded further, can generate videos from text and images. Recently, Runway has also been updated to include 'motion brushes', which allow you to select a particular part of an image and add motion just to that element, such as a bird turning its head, or a ship on a rolling ocean. Both platforms currently generate very short clips of around four seconds in duration.

Creating clips from text and images

The difference between using a text prompt and an image prompt in both platforms is that text prompts give a 'classic' image-generation experience, whereas image prompts will add (generally quite subtle) movement to an existing image. There's a place for both approaches. Runway's text-to-video is pretty impressive, although it does struggle with complex generations and lots of movement. Again, you should check out the blog post (or better yet, try the applications themselves) for the full experience.

Pika has a similar approach, and also borrows a few terms from other image-generation platforms like Midjourney for controlling things like aspect ratio (the width and height of the videos). You have more control over the visual style with an image-based prompt, but less control over the movement. For example, you can generate an image in an image generator like DALL·E 3, Adobe Firefly, Bing Image Creator or Midjourney, and add some movement to the image.

Making an entire video

Obviously, you can't do much with a 3–4 second clip, but it's not difficult to generate a few scenes and stitch them together in any video-editing software. Because I'm trying to learn it myself, I used Adobe Premiere Pro in the original blog post, but that's definitely overcomplicating things. I've also stitched videos together and added audio using TikTok on my phone, and there are hundreds of free apps out there that would allow you (or your students) to do the same. In the post, I made a video 'advertising' lemon and ginger tea (because that's what I was drinking when I decided to make the video…).

The videos were generated through a combination of text- and image-to-video prompts in Pika. I used Pika because, unlike Runway, I wasn't running out of generation credits. Here is the process I followed:

1. Generate still images (the cup of tea, the packet of tea at the end) in Midjourney.
2. Generate videos with text-to-video in Pika (shots of lemons, shots of ginger).
3. Generate videos with image-to-video in Pika.

4. Drag and drop clips into the correct order in Premiere Pro and slow some clips down to extend the length of time.
5. Add a couple of basic transitions and text in Premiere Pro.
6. Generate an audio track in Stable Audio and add it to the video in Premiere Pro.
7. Export the finished movie.

The future of video generation

As video generation continues to improve, we will see entirely AI-generated animations, short films and advertisements become the norm. Eventually, television-length and then feature-length films will be created entirely using AI; in fact, that's part of Runway's mission statement.

This obviously has huge implications for the film, advertising and other creative industries that some of our students might be interested in entering as they finish school. As I said in chapter 29, however, it doesn't mean there's no place for human artists and creatives in these industries. There are many complex creative, ethical and legal aspects that we'll need to navigate in the next few years before AI video generation becomes an industry standard, and along the way, students will still need to develop the necessary core skills, whatever their pathways.

CHAPTER 33
3D asset generation

Using similar technologies to image generation, it is already possible to create three-dimensional 'assets' that can be imported into 3D and games development software. At the moment, it looks a little like the kind of 3D you might see in a video game from the 2000s, rather than something you'd expect to pop up in a Meta Quest virtual reality headset. But give it time...

Figure 12: 'An anime cat' generated in Luma AI

The 3D cat on the previous page was generated in a couple of seconds using Luma Labs' platform (another one that currently lives in Discord – I really wish they wouldn't...). Similar platforms are working on the same technology, including a research partnership between Adobe and Australian National University (Hong et al., 2023).

The obvious intent of text-to-3D is to create objects that can be used in video games, virtual reality and augmented or mixed reality. But instead of limiting this technology to games, think of the applications for everyday use in all kinds of industries. Soon enough, you'll be able to conjure up three-dimensional objects that appear instantly in front of your (augmented reality, glasses-wearing) eyes. You could also generate entire 3D environments in a full virtual reality platform. These technologies could be used for storytelling, workplace training or medical purposes. Or, more likely, they could be used for advertising and social media. Just like all the other technologies covered in this book, there are positives and negatives.

CHAPTER 34
Code generation

Code generation predates ChatGPT, but hasn't made a huge splash in education simply because not a lot of teachers code. Increasingly, though, these technologies can be used via natural language prompts to create fully functional software. This means that soon you'll be able to type (or speak) to an application that creates a working app in minutes or even seconds.

Right now, you can use GitHub Copilot (owned by Microsoft), ChatGPT, Google's Bard chatbot and a variety of other LLM-based applications to generate – and in some cases execute – code in many languages. Programming languages, just like written and spoken human languages, form a large part of LLM datasets. Some, like GitHub's, are specifically trained on code and finetuned to produce code in ways which exceed the skills of more general-purpose models like ChatGPT.

Programming languages like Python, HTML, CSS, JavaScript and C++ can all be generated with these models, meaning you can theoretically build applications, plugins, websites and all manner of software even with very low levels of technical understanding. In my experience, it's not yet possible to code fully-fledged and complex apps without *some* technical understanding, but that will change over time.

In my own experiments, I've created websites from sketches using ChatGPT's image recognition, generated working models of physics experiments with code interpreter, and built very simple games and applications.

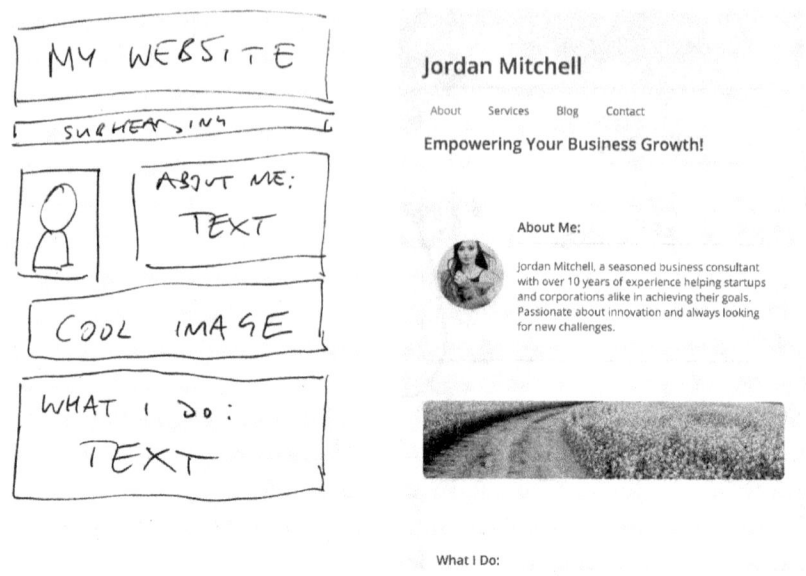

Figure 13: Sketch-to-website with ChatGPT (Plus)

I even used code generation in the creation of this book, as I briefly outlined on page xi. For example, I prompted ChatGPT to write a piece of software in Python that could 'scrape' my blog – specifically all the posts in the AI category – and convert the posts into Microsoft Word documents without the images, hyperlinks or other online features. I also worked with the code until it could format the documents with correct Word-style features, such as headings and lists. This meant that I was able to quickly create a table of contents for this book based on all of those original posts and gave me more than 20,000 words of draft material to work with.

I also created a very simple program that stitched together the various sections into a complete manuscript. When I write books, I tend to have each chapter and sometimes each sub-chapter in a separate Word document. In the past, I've then laboriously copy/pasted each chapter into a compiled doc. Now, I have a piece of software I (or ChatGPT) wrote that can do it in seconds.

```python
import requests
from bs4 import BeautifulSoup
from bs4.element import NavigableString
from docx import Document

# Function to add formatted text to a Word document
def add_formatted_text(paragraph, soup_element):
    for part in soup_element.contents:
        if isinstance(part, NavigableString):
            paragraph.add_run(str(part))
        else:
            style = None
            if part.name == 'strong' or part.name == 'b':
                style = 'bold'
            elif part.name == 'em' or part.name == 'i':
                style = 'italic'
            elif part.name == 'u':
                style = 'underline'

            run = paragraph.add_run(str(part.string))
            if style == 'bold':
                run.bold = True
            elif style == 'italic':
                run.italic = True
            elif style == 'underline':
                run.underline = True
            add_formatted_text(paragraph, part)

# Function to process each blog post
def process_blog_post(url):
    response = requests.get(url)
    soup = BeautifulSoup(response.content, 'html.parser')
    content = soup.find('div', class_='entry-content')
    doc = Document()
```

Figure 14: Example of the code generated to scrape blog posts for the draft of this book

CHAPTER 35
Bringing it all together

Now I've outlined image, text, audio, video, 3D assets and code generation, I want you to extrapolate each of these technologies further and imagine that they are progressing towards one another on a timeline.

Imagine a platform having all of these capabilities built into one place, starting with speech recognition already available in both the free and paid versions of ChatGPT. You will interact with this platform verbally (or in writing, if you choose). Using speech-to-text technologies, the model will interpret your instructions and can be used to create new data in multimodal forms. For example, using a combination of image, video and audio, you could verbally instruct the model to create a short educational video explaining a concept.

You could easily record an audio file of yourself speaking and have it converted into a talking avatar video. You can already do this now with platforms like HeyGen, but in the future, you'll do this all in one place. By extending it out a little further, you'll be able to instruct the model to create 3D assets and environments rendered in real time while you're wearing augmented or virtual reality gear. Imagine sitting in a chair at home and conjuring up virtual reality environments just by speaking into your headset or glasses. Again, this sounds like science fiction, but when Apple releases its virtual reality product and software, we've seen from the experience of the iPhone that there will be a huge explosion of these technologies' processing power and speed combined with generative multimodal capabilities.

Finally, let's bring in the code interpreter capabilities of a model like GPT. Again, interacting verbally or in writing with the model, you will be able to design, develop and deploy software applications for a variety of devices with a clearer understanding of the application. Even people with limited or no coding experience will be able to create software very rapidly. Again, this might sound like something that's far away in the future, but think back to the previous chapter where I created a couple of pieces of cheap and cheerful software to help compile this book. Whenever you have a digital problem to solve, I believe that multimodal GenAI will allow us to build those solutions on the fly.

Autonomous agents

If anything in this book is suggestive of science fiction, it's the idea of *autonomous agents*. Even writing about this, I feel like I'm laying the groundwork for a speculative fiction short story. Over the past 12 months, there have been a lot of debates about whether GenAI can be called conscious, whether it can have agency and whether it can be considered to have 'personhood'. Let's go back to the earlier section on multimodality for a second; some of this is a just problem with definitions.

What does 'agency' actually mean? Some people think that agency means AI needs to be able to act by itself. Others think agency simply means it has the capacity to *influence* other people's actions. If the latter is true, then GenAI does have a certain amount of agency. All technology can be considered 'agentic' in some capacity. You might think of PowerPoint as a neutral application, but think about the influence that slideshows have had on the way we communicate (especially in boring meetings). Similarly, think about how Zoom has changed meetings since COVID-19, both for good and for bad. GenAI is similarly agentic: these applications influence the way we produce texts in many ways. Although it's still the user controlling the model, it's the algorithm and training on the dataset which exerts control over the output.

At the time of writing, AI systems aren't truly autonomous, in that they need to be developed and used by humans with human intent. However, there is increasing speculation and work being done by AI companies to produce autonomous AI agents that can act for themselves and interact with one another. Prominent people in the fields of technology, including Bill Gates and the CEO of OpenAI, Sam Altman, have suggested that autonomous AI agents or assistants are very near and very likely to emerge from current generations of AI technology.

In education, the implications are huge. At the moment, 'personalised learning' is a buzzword being touted by EdTech companies, but it's mostly more of a marketing tool than an actual product. But when GenAI is combined with predictive algorithms that can track every aspect of our lives, including the ways we interact with learning materials, then it might be a possibility. The question is: do we want that?

Conclusion

I began this book by talking about my PhD studies, and why I decided to get into the field of GenAI. I was, and still am, hopeful about the creative potential of GenAI for both educators and students. In order to realise that creative potential, we need some serious effort to be put into resourcing and training over the next few years. It doesn't matter that the technology is moving so fast or that there are thousands of new apps every week – we need to make sure educators have the fundamental skills to work with GenAI.

Hopefully I've covered many of those fundamental skills. I began with a technical discussion of GenAI because I think it's important that we know exactly what we're dealing with, how it's made and where all that data comes from. Then I focused on ethics because I firmly believe we can't bring GenAI into classrooms until we know the risks – particularly in terms of bias and marginalisation.

But getting up on the ethical high horse doesn't mean ignoring, banning or railing against the technology. GenAI will be used in ways which are harmful, destructive and cause chaos. We have a responsibility to our students to help them – and ourselves – learn as much as we can.

In her excellent book, *12 Bytes*, author Jeanette Winterson wrote the following:

> *"As the reptile brain of the alt right seeks to reshape the world as medieval serfdom for the many, with a tech Nirvana for the few, liberal resistance can't be anti-tech or anti-science, even while we rightly protest about surveillance, about data harvesting, about the cruel land grab of what should be free and meaningful worldwide connectivity."*

As an educator, and particularly an English and Literature teacher, I've always kind of seen myself as part of the 'liberal resistance'. But I've also been a student of computer science and a user of technologies. I've built websites and played with code and enjoyed using GenAI, including before, during and after the wave of hype that crashed over us in November 2022.

I want you to leave this book prepared to experience some of that joy, and some of the fear and anxiety, and all of the other emotions associated with this complex, powerful technology.

References

Australian Curriculum, Assessment and Reporting Authority (ACARA). (2023). *Artificial intelligence (AI)*. V9 Australian Curriculum. v9.australiancurriculum.edu.au/teacher-resources/understand-this-curriculum-connection/artificial-intelligence

Briggs, J., & Kodnani, D. (2023). *The Potentially Large Effects of Artificial Intelligence on Economic Growth*. Goldman Sachs. www.key4biz.it/wp-content/uploads/2023/03/Global-Economics-Analyst_-The-Potentially-Large-Effects-of-Artificial-Intelligence-on-Economic-Growth-Briggs_Kodnani.pdf

Deloitte Australia. (2023). 'Generation AI: Ready or not, here we come!' | Deloitte Australia. www.deloitte.com/au/en/services/consulting/analysis/generation-ai-ready-or-not.html

Department of Education, C. C. (2023). The Australian Framework for Generative Artificial Intelligence (AI) in Schools. www.education.gov.au/schooling/announcements/australian-framework-generative-artificial-intelligence-ai-schools

Donahoe, E. P. (2023). 'The Rise of Generative AI Calls for New Approaches to Grading.' *Unmaking the Grade*. emilypittsdonahoe.substack.com/p/the-rise-of-generative-ai-calls-for

Duffy, C., & Stewart, J. (2022). 'Investigation reveals tracking by EdTech of millions of Australian school students during COVID lockdowns.' ABC News. www.abc.net.au/news/2022-05-25/investigation-reveals-educational-tech-tracking-children-data/101091808

Elkhoury, E. (2023). *Types of Oral Assessments*. Athabasca University. alternative-assessment.com/wp-content/uploads/2023/09/Types-of-Oral-Assessments-.pdf

Franzetti, S. (2023). 'Learning Conferences as a Humanizing Evaluation Practice.' *Zeal: A Journal for the Liberal Arts, 1*(2).

Furze, L. (2023). *VINE Generative Artificial Intelligence Guidelines*. Victorian ICT Network for Education. vine.vic.edu.au/resources/Documents/GAI_Guidelines/VINE%20Generative%20Artificial%20Intelligence%20Guidelines.pdf

Goldstein, J. A., Sastry, G., Musser, M., DiResta, R., Gentzel, M., & Sedova, K. (2023). 'Generative Language Models and Automated Influence Operations: Emerging Threats and Potential Mitigations.' doi.org/10.48550/ARXIV.2301.04246

Hong, Y., Zhang, K., Gu, J., Bi, S., Zhou, Y., Liu, D., Liu, F., Sunkavalli, K., Bui, T., & Tan, H. (2023). 'LRM: Large Reconstruction Model for Single Image to 3D.' doi.org/10.48550/ARXIV.2311.04400

Kress, G. (2003). *Literacy in the New Media Age*. Routledge.

Kress, G. (2010). *Multimodality: A social semiotic approach to contemporary communication.* Routledge.

Luccioni, A. S., Jernite, Y., & Strubell, E. (2023). 'Power Hungry Processing: Watts Driving the Cost of AI Deployment?' doi.org/10.48550/ARXIV.2311.16863

McKinsey & Company. (2023). *Generative AI and the future of work in America.* McKinsey. www.mckinsey.com/mgi/our-research/generative-ai-and-the-future-of-work-in-america

Perkins, M., Furze, L., Roe, J., & MacVaugh, J. (2023). 'Navigating the generative AI era: Introducing the AI assessment scale for ethical GenAI assessment.' doi.org/10.48550/arXiv.2312.07086

Perrigo, B. (2023). 'OpenAI Used Kenyan Workers on Less Than $2 Per Hour.' *Time* magazine. time.com/6247678/openai-chatgpt-kenya-workers/

Reisner, A. (2023). 'Revealed: The Authors Whose Pirated Books Are Powering Generative AI.' *The Atlantic.* www.theatlantic.com/technology/archive/2023/08/books3-ai-meta-llama-pirated-books/675063/

Strubell, E., Ganesh, A., & McCallum, A. (2019). 'Energy and Policy Considerations for Deep Learning in NLP.' doi.org/10.48550/ARXIV.1906.02243

UNESCO. (2023). 'Guidance for generative AI in education and research.' www.unesco.org/en/articles/guidance-generative-ai-education-and-research

Whitney, L. (2023). *How to access thousands of free audiobooks, thanks to Microsoft AI and Project Gutenberg.* ZDNET. www.zdnet.com/article/heres-how-to-access-thousands-of-free-audiobooks-thanks-to-microsoft-ai-and-project-gutenberg

Yang, C., Wang, X., Lu, Y., Liu, H., Le, Q. V., Zhou, D., & Chen, X. (2023). 'Large Language Models as Optimizers.' doi.org/10.48550/ARXIV.2309.03409

Further reading

It's impossible to cover the depth and breadth of AI in any single book. Over the course of my studies, I've come across some amazing and accessible books which explore the technical, ethical and practical concerns of AI. These include GenAI, but also go much broader and into areas like predictive algorithms, privacy and the future of our lives with technology.

Here are a handful of suggestions for further reading:

- Buolamwini, Joy – *Unmasking AI*
- Crawford, Kate – *Atlas of AI*
- Kasparov, Garry – *Deep Thinking*
- Lee, Kai-Fu (trans. Chen Qiufan) – *AI 2041*
- Li, Fei-Fei – *The Worlds I See*
- Spicer, Tracey – *Man-Made*
- Srnicek, Nick – *Platform Capitalism*
- Winterson, Jeanette – *12 Bytes*
- Zuboff, Shoshana – *The Age of Surveillance Capitalism*

GenAI apps and services

By the time you're reading this, some of these could have come and gone – it's moving so quickly that you're better off learning to approach the technology as a whole rather than specific apps. These are the apps either referenced in this book, or which I currently use:

Text generation
- ChatGPT – chat.openai.com
- Google Bard – bard.google.com/chat
- Microsoft Bing Chat – www.bing.com/new
- Anthropic Claude – claude.ai
- HuggingChat – huggingface.co/chat

Image generation
- Microsoft Bing Image Creator (DALL·E 3) – www.bing.com/images/create
- Adobe Firefly – firefly.adobe.com
- Clipdrop (Stable Diffusion) – clipdrop.co
- Midjourney – midjourney.com

Audio generation
- Stable Audio – www.stableaudio.com
- ElevenLabs – elevenlabs.io
- Google MusicLM – blog.google/technology/ai/musiclm-google-ai-test-kitchen

Video generation
- Runway – runwayml.com
- Pika – pika.art/login

3D generation
- Luma AI – lumalabs.ai

About the author

Leon Furze is an international consultant, author, and speaker with over fifteen years of experience in secondary and tertiary education and leadership. Leon is studying his PhD in the implications of Generative Artificial Intelligence on writing instruction and education.

Leon has held roles at multiple levels of school and board leadership, including Director of Teaching and Learning, Head of English, and eLearning. Leon is a Non-Executive Director on the board of Young Change Agents and Reframing Autism, and a member of Council for the Victorian Association for the Teaching of English.

Leon completed his Master of Education at the University of Melbourne in 2016 with a focus on student wellbeing, leading schools through change, and linking education systems and communities. He has published dozens of books, articles and courses, with his most recent publications, *Practical Reading Strategies* and *Practical Writing Strategies* reaching an international audience.

Leon presents at state and national conferences and runs online and face to face professional learning for schools, individuals and businesses. Through consultancy and advisory work, Leon helps educators from K-12 to tertiary to understand the implications of Generative Artificial Intelligence in education.

www.ingramcontent.com/pod-product-compliance
Lightning Source LLC
Chambersburg PA
CBHW052131110526
44591CB00012B/1674